DIVIDENDS TO PAY

E. D. KENNEDY

DIVIDENDS TO PAY

REPRINTS OF ECONOMIC CLASSICS

AUGUSTUS M. KELLEY · PUBLISHERS
NEW YORK 1969

First Edition 1939
(New York: Reynal & Hitchcock, 1939)

Reprinted 1969 by
Augustus M. Kelley • Publishers
New York New York 10010
By Arrangement with HARCOURT, BRACE & WORLD, INC.

SBN 678 00522 2

Library of Congress Catalogue Card Number
68–56239

PRINTED IN THE UNITED STATES OF AMERICA
by SENTRY PRESS, NEW YORK, N. Y. 10019

For Elizabeth

CONTENTS

INTRODUCTION

EVER SINCE the October, 1929, break in the stock market, people have been talking about recovery. There was the Hoover period, in which "prosperity was right around the corner." There was the first Roosevelt Administration, in which the President checked the progress of depression but in which industry, through its failure to restore employment, prevented the recovery movement from acquiring a substantial basis. And, finally, there was the "recovery" of 1936–1937. Here, through the payment of the soldiers' bonus, along with continued relief expenditures, a considerable amount of money was put into circulation and the foundation for a genuine recovery was laid. But the industrialist, in too great a hurry to pick up where he had left off in 1929, stepped up prices and production too rapidly for the still weakened purchasing power of the public to absorb his output. As a consequence, the depression again took on one of its acute phases and industry is now having another bad year. But people still talk about recovery, although now they are dating it in 1939.

If by recovery is meant a movement back to the conditions of 1929, with no change in the underlying factors prevailing at that time, a return to 1929 would only be a preliminary to a return to 1932. Indeed, I suspect that the historian of the future will refer to the 1920's, and certainly to the last half of that decade, as the "pre-depression" period in American economic history. Those years, so commonly remembered as a period of great prosperity, are better described as a period of great activity. The prosperity (as I shall show later) was highly selective — a few persons amassed great fortunes, but the time was remarkable for the accumulation rather than for the distribution of wealth.

In 1929, for example, there were 14,800 persons with individual incomes of more than $100,000 a year. The total income of these persons was $4,400,000,000. They took in more than one-third as much money as 8,800,000 factory workers collected in wages for the year. They took in over four-fifths as much money as was paid to about 4,500,000 persons employed in retail trade. The average annual wage in manufacturing for that year was $1320. The average annual wage in retailing was about $1180. But the persons in the over-$100,000 a year income class averaged about $300,000 per man. The total national income for that year, estimated by the Department of Commerce, was $81,000,000,000. And here we have 14,800 persons with a cash income equivalent to more than one-twentieth of that amount. Under these circumstances, it is not surprising that the ability of industry to produce outstripped the ability of the public to buy.

This book, however, is not a study of individual incomes. Discrepancies in individual incomes are commonly – though vaguely – realized. I have approached the subject of depressions and recoveries through a study of *corporate* income. There are a great many unincorporated businesses in this country, but they are mostly small businesses. The significant movements in trade and commerce are comprehensively reflected in corporate reports. I believe, also, that the subject of business in general has not been previously approached through the specific study of corporations specified by name.

And it is essential to be specific. In speaking about profits, it should be mentioned that General Motors has made $1,028,000,000 *since* 1929 and paid out $948,000,000 in dividends during the depression years. In discussing prices, it seems to me desirable to point out that since 1926 sulphur has sold for $18 a barrel, f.o.b. New Orleans, and that the major producers of sulphur in this country are the Texas Gulf Sulphur and the Freeport Sulphur companies. In talking of companies controlled by banking-houses, I consider it helpful to know that in 1927 J. P. Morgan and Co. bought 400,000 of the 750,000 shares of Johns-Manville stock then outstanding. I have, however, referred to specific companies only to illustrate general conditions. This is not a book about individual companies. It is a book about the industrial system as a whole.

The first section of the book establishes the statistical basis. The figures are from the U. S. Treasury Department's *Statistics of Income* and from a compilation, made by the Standard Statistics Co., of the reports of 960 large corporations. In it we shall see that, although there are 475,000 corporations in the United States, a few large companies like those just mentioned have been monopolizing the *profits* of industry since even before the depression era. The illusion that corporate dividends make a major contribution to the support of "millions" of middle-class Americans who are also "partners" in American industry is also examined, with the conclusion that dividends are in reality a factor not in the distribution but in the concentration of wealth.

The second section is less statistical and more descriptive. In *Multiple Monopoly* I have tried to show why the existence of two or more large companies in the same field is no guarantee of genuine competition among them. In *The Price Umbrella* I have discussed price "stabilization" in the steel industry since the formation of U. S. Steel. *The Decline of the Corporate Manager* considers the extent to which the president of the contemporary large corporation has been reduced to the position of a hired hand. And in *Overproduction and Underconsumption* I have taken the automobile industry as an example of the fact that, although the problem of mass production was solved in the 1920's, the 1930's have made very little headway with the resulting problem of mass sales.

In the final section, I have been chiefly concerned with the relations between business and society. I believe that, in the last stages of the "prosperity" era, business got itself badly overcapitalized, not with respect to its assets but with respect to its market. To secure for its investors a satisfactory return on their investment, industry was compelled to market a tremendous volume of commodities, priced to yield a high profit per unit sale. When, late in 1929, it became evident that this dollar volume could be no longer sustained, the industrialist reduced his output. In order to maintain his profit — which means, in the contemporary large corporations, to pay his dividends — the corporate manager reduced his costs, chiefly by firing a large portion of the men who worked for him. (Wages in manufacturing in 1933 were some 45% of what they had been in 1929.) As unemployment increased, the purchasing power of the public decreased, so that even the reduced output of industry was still too great for the market to absorb. This process (commonly known as the *depression spiral*) continued under Mr. Hoover until it brought on the bank holiday under Mr. Roosevelt. But in spite of Mr. Roosevelt's efforts (and the New Deal has been the only factor of salvation in this country for the past six years), industry has continued to operate on an "economy" basis and unemployment has not been below the 7,500,000 mark since the 1930 wave of unemployment set in. In 1937, industry became briefly expansive, but, as I have already suggested, expanded more rapidly than the financial condition of the public justified. Now industry is back in the doldrums again, and some 4,000,000 persons who had jobs in the early fall of 1937 are lacking jobs today.

And the money-saving, cost-cutting attitude of industry shows every promise of being its permanent point of view. The industrialist of today is not interested in expanding his capacity — he already has far too much capacity for his own good. He is not interested in making jobs. Most of his depression expenditures have been in the way of buying new machinery with which further to lessen his labor costs. By keeping costs — particularly payroll costs — to a minimum, the monopoly-corporation can make a profit under almost any conditions of general trade. But in cutting costs, the industrialist reduces the income, not only of the worker, but of the public as a whole. For the jobless man is bad for business and it does not take many millions of jobless men to make all business bad.

We are, therefore, threatened with a permanent depression — a depression for which the ground was being broken at least as far back as 1925. During the 1920's the accumulation of wealth so far outstripped the distribution of wealth as to set up an unbalance which has not yet been restored. Long before 1929 the great mass of American corporations which still do business on a competitive basis were faced with dwindling profits, although this condition was obscured by the rapidly mounting profits of a few large monopolistic companies whose greatly increased profits produced a deceptive appearance of prosperity all around. Since 1929 the competitive corporations have, as a unit, accumulated appalling deficits in almost every year. But the thousand or so monopolistic companies at the top of the industrial heap have never, as a unit, lost a cent. And the bulk of the stock in these few corporations is owned by a few thousand large stockholders, already rich but determined to increase their riches at no matter what damage to the general good.

A few companies make the profits; a few people own most of the few companies that make the profits. I do not claim this as an original discovery, but I have tried to document it in a manner that will take it out of the realm of controversy and establish it in the realm of fact. Furthermore, it is not commonly realized *how* few companies make *how much* of the money, and *how* few their large stockholders are. Nor do I think the great difference between the expanding industrialist of 1929 and the contracting industrialist of 1939 is generally appreciated. In 1929 the industrialist sincerely considered himself an asset to the community and the community, for the most part, agreed with him. Now his position as a liability is becoming constantly more apparent, but this is a development which he can hardly avoid. He would prefer to be popular. And it is both embarrassing and expensive for him to be so unpopular that his political ally has been the minority party since Mr. Roosevelt's election in 1932. By proclaiming himself the only true American and with the assistance of that portion of the Democratic party for which the New Deal has no attraction, he hopes to remedy his situation in 1940. But although the industrialist's interest in society has not diminished, it now finds difficulty even in masquerading as the benevolent interest for which it was once commonly mistaken. The monopoly industrialist once said to the public, "Let's you *and* I prosper side by side." He is now, however, approaching the point at which, if he spoke truthfully, he would be saying, "Let's you *or* I prosper by ourselves." He has dividends to pay.

Chapter I

THE FEW VERSUS THE MANY: BY CORPORATIONS

In 1925 there were about 385,000 corporations in the United States. The number had risen to 456,000 in 1929* and is somewhat in excess of that figure today. Taken as a whole, the corporations make up the great body of American business. For although there are many businesses which are not incorporated — including some 1,500,000 small retail stores — these businesses are not large enough to exert much influence on the state of trade. Industry in this country has become so largely Industry, Inc., that the condition of the whole can be accurately measured by the condition of its incorporated part. It would be difficult, although not impossible, for *all* the corporations to be prosperous without some measure

* In 1929 there was a total of 509,400 companies, of which 53,400 were inactive. Figures used throughout for number of corporations are for *active* corporations. Since no breakdown of active and inactive companies is available for 1925 and 1926, estimates have been made on the basis of 1927, 1928, and 1929 ratios.

of prosperity extending to the people as a whole.

But there never has been a time in American business history when all the corporations were prosperous. Even during the best years of the 1920's, a little less than two companies out of every five were reporting deficits. As Coolidge prosperity turned into Hoover prosperity, as the output of industry reached higher and higher totals and the stock market rose to more and more speculative heights, it was becoming constantly more difficult for 99 out of every 100 companies to make any profits at all. The corporate prosperity of the 1920's was a very selective, almost an exclusive, prosperity. It belonged to relatively few high-profit corporations and its major beneficiaries were relatively few rich men. The period was marked by great *activity*, but the profits resulting from this activity were not widely enough distributed to create a general prosperity even in the business world. Since 1929, more than three companies out of every five have lost money every year. Yet essentially the same group of companies which made most of the money during the 1920's have continued to make large profits during the depression years. From 1930 through 1937, for example, the General Motors company had made more than one billion dollars in profits and paid almost $950,000,000 in dividends.

During the boom period the prevailing opinion was that all corporations were prosperous. During the depression, the prevailing opinion has been that all corporations have been showing deficits. These are fundamental errors and any attempt to reason from them leads to a false conclusion. They arise from the habit of considering all corporations as a unit. They are based on the statistics of income of all companies. The company which makes $10,000,000 a year is considered as being no more significant than the company which makes $1,000 a year. If the profits of all the companies that make money are considerably greater than the losses of all the companies that lose money, the conclusion is that business is good. If the profits of the profit-making companies are not as great as the losses of the deficit-making companies, the conclusion is that business is bad. The fact is that, since 1925 at least, business has always been good for a few companies but for the great majority business has *not* been good.

The only source of figures on the income of all corporations is the Bureau of Internal Revenue of the U. S. Treasury Department. Every corporation has to file an income report along with its annual corporation income tax statement. Even companies with deficits for the year have to report their losses. The Internal Revenue Bureau publishes annually a summary of these reports, not only giving total figures but also listing income by income classes.* Most of the companies also turn in a balance sheet statement showing total assets, capitalization, funded debt, and other vital statistics. The Government counts the corporate noses very carefully and all the figures cited below which have to do with income or deficit of all corporations are taken from its *Statistics of Income.* The Government is, however, a very slow counter. As these lines are being written (July, 1939), a preliminary report for 1935 is the latest Treasury bulletin on perhaps the most vital subject that any Federal department has to issue reports about. With this qualification, however, the *Statistics of Income* remain as the complete and official statements on the status of American corporate life.

It is from these statistics, to be sure, that apologists for our economic system took the misleading, all-inclusive figures to which reference has already been made. The false impression, however, cannot be blamed on the Treasury as the same statistics, more carefully studied, clearly demonstrate the unsound character of the superficial inferences so often drawn from them. Let us first

---

* For example, in 1929, 69,500 companies reported a net income of less than $1,000; 110,200 companies reported a net income of between $1,000 and $5,000; and so on up through companies reporting a net of $5,000,000 & over. Deficits are similarly listed by classes.

quote the figures in the form which made them so popular with the business man, the newspapers, and the public during the second half of the 1920's. The following table shows the net income (profits of the money-makers minus losses of the money-losers) of all corporations from 1925 through 1929.

Year	All Corps.	Net Income
1925	385,000	$7,620,000,000
1926	407,500	7,500,000,000
1927	425,700	6,510,000,000
1928	443,600	8,230,000,000
1929	456,000	8,740,000,000

It is easy to see why Coolidge and Hoover and Mellon and his aid Ogden Mills were so fond of figures like these. They were the statistical basis for the conclusion that the prosperity of the period was very well founded. They indicated that during these five years more and more companies were making more and more money, the profit for 1929 being about one billion dollars greater than the profit for 1925. Yet the increase was not so great as to suggest an inflated prosperity — a peak period to be followed by a crash. Indeed, the industrialist of 1929 was not so proud of his prosperity as he was of what he considered to be the *stability* of his prosperity. He did not believe that profits were increasing at any dangerous rate, for the extra billion dollars made in 1929 over 1925 could be attributed to the fact there were some 70,000 more corporations in the latter year. Indeed, in both 1925 and 1929 the "average" corporate profit was a little less than $20,000 a year. So it was concluded that all the companies, as a group, were doing well, but that they were not doing too well. And — until the autumn of 1929 — the general opinion was not only that the United States was an extremely prosperous country, but that it would in every likelihood continue to be an extremely prosperous country for a great many years to come.

Yet if anyone had taken the trouble to look beyond the figures for all corporations and to study some of the figures on income by income classes, he could perhaps have shaken even the Nineteen-Twenty-Niner's confidence in Nineteen-Twenty-Nine. For he would have seen that a little more than 1,000 corporations in the class of corporations with a net income of more than $1,000,000 a year were making an extraordinarily high percentage of the profits of all corporations. He would have seen that the income of these million-dollar-a-year companies was increasing in a most dangerously inflationary manner, particularly in 1926 and 1929. He would have realized that a handful of tremendously profitable corporations were getting a strangle-hold on the profits of industry as a whole and that, aside from the numerically insignificant group of big winners, the remaining companies were reporting, as a group, small and constantly decreasing profits.

The following table shows the number of companies with a net income of $1,000,000 or more a year, the total net income of this group, and the percentage of the total income of this group to the total income of all corporations. The source is the same *Statistics of Income* from which the previous figures were taken:

Year	Corps. with $1,000,000 Net	Net Income of These Corps.	Proportion of Their Net to Net of All Corps.
1925	1,113	$4,970,000,000	65%
1926	1,097	5,240,000,000	70%
1927	1,024	4,640,000,000	71%
1928	1,258	5,930,000,000	72%
1929	1,349	7,000,000,000	80%

These figures show the extent to which the profits of all business were made up of the profits of a few great profit makers. The million-dollar companies are, by number, less than 0.3% (three-tenths of one per cent, or three out of one thousand) of all corporations. Yet in 1925 they made 65% of the net income of all corporations; that is, their profits were about twice the net income of all the other companies combined. And in 1929, when more companies were making more money, the million-dollar-profit companies made 80% of the total net — four times as much as all the other companies in the United States. It is true that there are no losers in the small group whereas the net income of the large group is a profit-minus-deficit figure.* Later, I shall make similar comparisons using a small group of so-called "representative" or "leading" companies which includes those with large losses as well as large gains. What I am now concerned with is the large amount of money made by a handful of high-profit companies and the small amount of money left over for all the other corporations to share.

The total income of the million-dollar-profit companies increased from 1925 through 1929 by about 40%. The actual money increase was a little over two billion dollars. We have already seen that the "average" profit of all corporations in both years was not quite $20,000. But in the million-dollar group the average profit was $4,-400,000 in 1925 and $5,200,000 in 1929.

We have seen the financial record of "all corporations" and the financial record of corporations

* See Appendix A, page 274, for a tabulation of the total profits of *all corporations reporting profits* in the prosperity years, and the total deficit of all corporations reporting losses. Notice how the number of deficit-reporters steadily increased during these years—until in 1929 it was some 40% greater than in 1925; and how the number of profit-reporters increased barely 7% in the same period.

making $1,000,000 a year or more. Remember that the figures for the small group are included in the figures for all companies; that is, the $8,740,-000,000 net income of all corporations in 1929 includes the $7,000,000,000 made by the 1,349 companies in the million-dollar class. Now suppose we see what all the companies *except* these million-dollar companies did, as a group, during this period. Let us subtract the profits of the million-dollar companies from the profits of all companies and see what the remaining companies had left. And do not forget that this "remainder" constitutes about 997 out of every 1,000 corporations in the United States. Here is the record of all companies minus the big winners:

Year	All Corps. with Less Than $1,000,000 Net	Net Income of This Group	Net Income per Corp., This Group
1925	383,900	$2,650,000,000	$6,900
1926	406,400	2,260,000,000	5,500
1927	424,700	1,870,000,000	4,400
1928	442,300	2,300,000,000	5,200
1929	454,600	1,740,000,000	3,800

Now we can see how closely the prosperity of the 1920's resembled a slot machine, and how lean were the pickings for those companies that missed the jackpot. Although the net income of all companies increased about 15% in five years, and the net income of the million-dollar companies increased 40%, the net income of all these other companies was 35% *decreased*. The money shrinkage was almost one billion dollars. The average profit dropped from $6,900 to $3,800. This dollar figure, like all such mythical averages, is not particularly significant. But the decline is most significant indeed. For every $5 that this group of companies had made in 1925 they could show little more than $3 in 1929. The profits of more than 99% of all corporations were being cut more than a third during what are commonly considered the most prosperous years that American industry ever experienced.

The most vital point in these tables is not so much the size of the figures as the direction of the figures. While the profits of the few companies were going rapidly up, the profits of the many companies were going rapidly down. We should have expected a more rapid increase in the profits of the high-profit companies. We should perhaps have expected them to get most of the increase in the profits of all companies. But here we have not a discrepancy but a contradiction. The *more* money the few companies made, the *less* money the many companies made.

We have seen that the 1925–1929 increase in all corporate profits was about a billion dollars. If the big profit makers had absorbed this entire increase, they still could have added only a billion dollars to their profits. But in 1929 they made *two* billion dollars more than they had made in 1925. Where did the other billion dollars come from? It came from the decline in profits of all other companies – of the 454,600 corporations which in 1929 made a billion dollars less than 384,000 corporations had made in 1925. The rich companies were not sharing prosperity with the poor, or the moderately well off, or even the well-to-do companies. The rich companies were making money *at the expense of* the other companies. The top three-tenths of one per cent of the corporations had become a parasite on the corporate body as a whole.

For a long time the industrialist has argued that as the size of the pie increases, everybody must get a bigger slice. This is his only attempt to justify – from a social standpoint – the corporation with the million-dollar-a-year profit, just as it is his only attempt to justify the million-dollar-a-year income. But the larger pie means nothing when the fellow who had the biggest slice in the first place not only eats up all the increase, but even cuts into the small portion that the other fellows had before. During the latter part of the 1920's the accumulation of wealth by the few proceeded so much more rapidly than the distribution of wealth to the many that the benefits of increased national wealth were largely lost.

With the arrival of the depression, the net income of all the companies except the big profit-makers immediately turned into a net deficit — that is, the deficits of the companies outside the high-profit group were greater than the profits of the companies in that group.* But the group of million-dollar profit makers itself by no means disappeared. Even in 1932 there were 284 such companies, with a total profit of $1,247,000,000. It would therefore be possible to continue this discussion in terms of the Government's *Statistics of Income*, comparing the million-dollar profit makers with all the companies not in their select group. But these companies are not the same every year. Their number fluctuated sharply during the depression and the so-called recovery years. At

* In setting up the concept of these two groups, I am not attempting to convey to the reader the impression that every company outside the select group of heavy profit-makers lost money every year of the depression; or that every company in the top group made money every year. (In Appendix B, page 275, I have continued the tabulation of the actual number of profit-makers and loss-takers in these years, with the profits and deficits they reported.) What I am trying to show is that the unbalance of the prosperity years reached its climax in the depression years when a *part* of our corporate economy (the net income of the select group) was indeed greater than *the whole* of it (the net income of all corporations).

the low point (1932) they included too many public utility companies to constitute a truly representative group. And, as I have already said, the last Government income report is for 1935 and, being a preliminary report, does not include incomes by income classes.*

I am therefore substituting for the million-dollar profit makers another group of select corporations. I am going to cite the profits of a group of 960 companies whose earnings have been tabulated from 1926 through 1937 by the Standard Statistics Co. This company, as its name implies, is a statistical and investment service designed chiefly for persons interested in the stock market. Its figures, compiled directly from the reports of the companies themselves, are thoroughly reliable and the 960 companies are, in many ways, a better "sample" than the million-dollar profit makers listed by the government.

They are the same 960 companies for the entire twelve years. Among them are companies from every industry, including non-prosperous industries like construction, coal mining, shipping, and textiles. They are a better cross section of industry as a whole and, although most of the companies are big money-makers, the total profit

* In Appendix C, page 276, I have continued the comparison of all companies with the million-dollar group for as many years as these figures are available.

of the group allows for many large deficits, particularly in the worst stages of the depression years. But they remain a select group and in only one year (1932) did they fail to average a million dollars profit apiece. From an earnings standpoint, therefore, they are comparable with the top companies in the Government list. Standard Statistics does not identify them by name, but, broadly speaking, they comprise the 960 most active of the corporations listed on the New York Stock Exchange. (Some companies which are almost certain to be in the Standard Statistics group will be discussed specifically in the next chapter.)

The Government figures, however, remain the only source of income for all corporations, so that I am continuing to use the *Statistics of Income* to show what all but the 960 companies have been doing in the depression years. The 960 companies, like the million-dollar companies, are of course included in the reports of all companies, so by subtracting their totals from the totals of all companies we can continue to see how what is now the other 99.8% live.* In starting this new set of comparisons I should like to go back to 1926

---

* Companies do not report net income to the government on exactly the basis that they report to the stockholders, and there will be complaints that I am comparing figures which are not strictly comparable. But I am establishing broad, basic, and unmistakable trends. It is not the precise figures that are important. It is the relative magnitudes.

and show what the 960 companies did in 1926, 1927, 1928, and 1929. This will prevent a break in the continuity of the comparisons and give us the benefit of the full twelve years of statistics on the 960 Standard Statistics concerns.

From 1926 through 1929 the net income of the 960 companies was as follows:

Year	Net Income of 960 Companies
1926	$3,665,000,000
1927	3,290,000,000
1928	4,100,000,000
1929	4,740,000,000

For the same years the net income (already cited) of the Government's million-dollar group was:

Year	No. of Companies	Net Income
1926	1,097	$5,240,000,000
1927	1,024	4,640,000,000
1928	1,258	5,930,000,000
1929	1,349	7,000,000,000

The record of the 960 shows that the hand-picked character of the million-dollar-profit group did not distort our previous picture of the boom-time period. Their average net was $3,800,000 in 1926 and $4,900,000 in 1929 — 80% and 94%, respectively, of that of the companies in the Government group. Their profits per company, thus, were increasing even more rapidly than the profits per company in the government assortment. The closeness of resemblance between the two sets of figures, moreover, results from the presence in both the Government figures and the Standard Statistics figures of an ultra-select group of companies which figure a "normal" profit not in terms of $1,000,000 but in terms of $20,000,000 or more. There were some 70 such companies in 1929 and some 40 in 1937 and they represent the real cream of the corporate crop. In the next chapter we shall see what a large percentage of the profits even of the most profitable companies these aristocrats among the aristocrats turned in. For the time being, however, let us follow the 960 Standard Statistics companies, and all the other companies, through the depression years.

Let us first look at the 1930–1932 period – the three years during which (under a rock-ribbed Republican administration) the depression not only appeared but grew rapidly into a panic. Here is the net income of all corporations (Government figures) for these years:

Year	All Corporations	Net Income
1930	463,000	$1,550,000,000
1931	459,700	def. 3,290,000,000
1932	451,800	def. 5,640,000,000

Here even the all-corporation figures show that the economic system has experienced a major calamity. But these figures are still misleading. They conceal the fact that the most profitable companies still made large profits, and they minimize the deficits accumulated by all other concerns.

Here is the record of the 960 Standard Statistics companies for the same years:

960 Corporations

Year	
1930	$2,920,000,000
1931	1,370,000,000
1932	363,500,000

Notice that in two of these three years the 960 companies still made better than a million dollars net income apiece; that even in 1932 they were averaging close to $400,000 net. Even when the rest of the country really was going to hell in a hack, these corporations still kept the wolf several hundred thousand dollars from the door. When you hear about terrible business deficits during the depression, be sure you know what part of business is being discussed. The select group of corporations did not have any deficits. From 1926 through 1929 they had made about $15,800,000,000. From 1930 through 1932 they managed to make $4,600,000,000 more.

To see where the depression was most depressing, we should look at the record of all the companies except the 960 companies. Here is what happened to this group of companies, which continue to make up about 998 out of every 1,000 in the country:

All Corporations except 960

Year	Number	Income
1930	462,000	*def.* $1,370,000,000
1931	458,700	*def.* 4,660,000,000
1932	450,800	*def.* 6,000,000,000

Even in 1930 these companies have a big deficit. In 1932, with the 960 companies still making $363,000,000, these companies lost six billion dollars. In the first three years of depression, these companies, as a group, lost almost four-fifths of all the profits they had made in the last four years of the boom. (Their net income, 1926–1929, was about fifteen billion dollars; their deficit, 1930–1932 was nearly twelve billion dollars.) Most of their prosperity profits were gone and what remained were dwindling fast.

Now let us look at the next phase of the depression, the 1933–35 period marked by the arrival of President Roosevelt and the New Deal. This was the period which opened with the bank holiday and included the A.A.A., the N.R.A., the abandoning of the gold standard, and the beginning of large expenditures for the relief of the unemployed. It was also the period during which the industrialist, thoroughly panic-stricken at the time of Mr. Roosevelt's inaugural address and for a brief period thoroughly convinced of the President's wisdom (especially as exemplified by the National Recovery Act with its Blue Eagle and its Hugh Johnson), finally decided that his system was not completely ruined and began rapidly reverting to type.

During these years the profit figures for all corporations acquired a deceptively healthy look:

All Corporations

Year	Number	Net Income
1933	446,800	def. $2,550,000,000
1934	469,800	94,000,000
1935	476,900	1,700,000,000

The all-corporation deficit has disappeared in 1934 and by 1935 a very considerable profit has taken its place. But remember that the big apples are still in the barrel.

Here is the record of the 960 corporations for the same years:

960 Corporations

Year	Net Income
1933	$1,000,000,000
1934	1,410,000,000
1935	1,970,000,000

These are the companies in which the recovery was concentrated. Even in 1933 they were back again to the million a year average net. They averaged over $2,000,000 apiece in 1935. They were already making nearly three-fifths as much as they had made in 1927. They were the companies that could have cheered about recovery, although they greatly preferred to groan about taxation. But they were the *only* companies, as a group, that could entertain any delusions about being on the road back to 1929. The only reason that all corporations appear again to be making a profit is that their figures include the figures of the choice 960. For here is the 1933–1935 record of all corporations with the 960 left out:

All Corporations except 960

Year	Number	Net Income
1933	445,800	def. $3,550,000,000
1934	468,800	def. 1,310,000,000
1935	475,900	def. 270,000,000

In 1935 these companies came closer to the break-even point — no doubt a great moral victory, but not much material comfort in view of the continued large losses in 1933 and 1934. These companies, which, as a group, had lost $12,000,000,000 from 1930 through 1932, lost another $5,000,000,000 from 1933 through 1935. That left them $17,000,000,000 in the red for the six depression years. During the same years, the 960 companies made $9,000,000,000. These large cumulative figures show most conclusively how extremely false is the impression created by looking at figures which lump all corporations together, regardless of earning power. According to these over-all figures, American industry lost some eight billion dollars during the depression. The figure, taken by itself, is a correct figure and unquestionably indicates the existence of prolonged hard times. But it does not show that about two-tenths of one percent of American industry *made* nine billion dollars during these years and that the other 99.8% lost not eight billion but seventeen billion dollars.

For the profits of the past three years there is no good statistical basis, since the Treasury has not got around to publishing its "all corporation" figures. But we do know a good deal about the profits of the few companies at the top of the heap. The Standard Statistics 960 companies made a very rapid forward movement in 1936, turning in a net income of almost $3,000,000,000. This profit represented a billion-dollar increase over 1935 and brought the companies back almost to their 1927 record and to nearly two-thirds of their profits for 1929. In 1937 they approached even closer, with a profit of $3,226,-000,000.

I do not think that the profits of all the other corporations showed any corresponding increase The recovery of 1936 and the boom of early 1937 were extremely selective. High earnings were confined almost entirely to a few basic producing industries — iron, steel, aluminum, nickel, petroleum, industrial chemicals, electrical equipment, farm machinery, automobiles and auto accessories. The situation in 1937 in many ways resembled the situation in 1929, except that the 1937 corporate recovery was much more selective even than the 1929 corporate prosperity. The "other" corporations may have succeeded in making a small net income in 1936 but in 1937 they certainly fell back to an even smaller net — if not a deficit. Most of them were caught with a large inventory of high-priced products which they could not get rid of at profitable figures. General Motors, for instance, made nearly as much money in 1937 as in 1936, but toward the end of the year General Motors *dealers* were practically giving away their cars.

But this chapter is primarily statistical and I do not want, at this point, to get into any extended argument about the pseudo-recovery in 1937. There was certainly no question about 1938. Even the highest profit makers are now making substantially reduced profits and it should by

this time be obvious that when the profits of the
top companies go down the profits of all other
companies go out. The income figures for 1938
closely resembled those for 1931 — reduced but
still substantial profits for 0.2% of the companies
and another huge deficit for the group of 99.8%
which have been accumulating deficits for the past
eight years.

It will, then, be seen that figures concerning
the profits of all corporations are misleading —
so misleading that they invariably lend themselves
to conclusions altogether contradictory to the
facts. By combining the high profits of a few
companies with the small profits or with the
deficits of many companies, the apologist for the
present system attains two ends at once. In the
first place, he disguises the losses of the many
companies by balancing them with the gains of
the few. In the second place, he disguises the
profits of the few companies by balancing them
with the losses of the many. In 1929 he concluded
that everyone was doing well — not so well as
to create fears about an inflation, but well enough
to encourage satisfaction all around. In 1938 he
concluded that everyone was in a terrible condition,
that business could not survive the (wholly im-

aginary) attacks made upon it by the Administration and that only the Republican Party could save the ship, if indeed the ship were not already sinking. As we have just seen, however, "everyone" was not doing well in 1929; and even in 1938 a majority of the industrialist's favorite companies were a long way from deficit's door. When a man says, "Business is good," be sure you know what part of business he is discussing. When he says, "Business is terrible," be sure that he is not holding out on you a few hundred or a few thousand exceptions to the prevailing rule.

Chapter II

THE BIGGEST OF THE BIG

IN THE previous chapter we have seen how the earning power of American industry has become concentrated in the hands of less than one thousand of our 475,000 corporations. It is sufficiently amazing that one out of every 475 companies should account for such a large proportion of the profits of American business. Even more amazing, however, is the presence, within this small group of large earners, of an even smaller group of even larger earners – the aristocrats of the corporate aristocracy, the biggest of the big. We have been speaking of companies which make a minimum of $1,000,000 a year and of companies which average around $4,000,000 or $5,000,000 a year in so-called normal times. We have, properly enough, regarded these companies as high earners. But there are corporations in this country which would regard earnings of *only* a million dollars as a calamity. There are companies which, year in and year out, average

twenty and thirty and forty million dollars a year
or more. For the purposes of this discussion I
have taken $20,000,000 as the minimum annual
profit for entrance into this truly exclusive corporate circle. The figure is arbitrary, but if it were
lowered to ten million, or even to fifteen million,
I should have so many companies to consider that
this chapter would grow into a book.

In 1929, as we have already seen, the net income
of all corporations was $8,740,000,000. The net
income of the 960 Standard Statistics corporations was $4,740,000,000. With these figures in
mind, let us see what some of the really big earners
did in the final year of the late boom. At the top
of the list come five corporations whose 1929 earnings were $100,000,000 or more:

General Motors	$248,300,000
American Telephone	217,100,000
U. S. Steel	197,600,000
Standard of New Jersey	120,900,000
Pennsylvania Railroad	101,400,000
Total	$885,300,000

It seems a bit superfluous to identify any of these
corporations. In view of what has been said about
monopoly capitalism versus competitive capitalism, however, it may be noticed that in 1929
General Motors made about 34% of all automobiles, American Telephone operated practically
all the telephones, U. S. Steel had about 40% of

the nation's steel capacity and the Pennsylvania belongs to the so-called "natural monopoly" group of public utility concerns.

Our immediate interest, however, is with the profits of these five companies. They totalled $885,300,000, which was 19% of the profits of the 960 Standard Statistics companies and over 10% of the net income of all corporations for the year. I do not quite know how to state these figures as emphatically as they should be stated. Five companies out of roughly 500,000 is one out of 100,000 and one out of 100,000 is one one-thousandth of one per cent. So from a percentage standpoint we can say that one one-thousandth of one per cent of the companies made ten per cent of the money. Or we might subtract 5 from the actual 456,000 and say that out of $100 of profits made by American companies in 1929, five made $10 and the other $455,995 made $90. At any rate, I think it is evident that we have here a remarkable example of the concentration of corporate profit.

In a sense, however, the fact that these five companies made 19% of what the 960 Standard Statistics companies made is even more extraordinary. We already know that the bulk of corporate earning power is monopolized by a small group of companies, but it is surprising to find that even in this group the "run of mine" concerns are dwarfed by the topmost earners. It would take 885 companies, each making $1,000,000 a year, to equal the earnings of these five corporations and we know that even in 1929 there were only about 1350 companies that did make a million or more. And when we can assign one-fifth of the profits of the 960 biggest companies to five of those companies, we can dispose of any attempt to argue that the profits of these companies are only proportional to their size. It has been claimed that the big corporations do "most of" the business and therefore "naturally" make most of the money. But no one could maintain that five out of 960 specimens of big business carry on so much of the nation's trade and commerce that they should make $1 for every $4 made by the other 955.

Following the five companies in the $100,000,000 class came eight companies in the over-$50,000,000 class. They were:

Standard of Indiana	$78,500,000
New York Central	78,300,000
E. I. Du Pont de Nemours	78,200,000
Anaconda Copper	69,100,000
General Electric	67,300,000
Consolidated Edison	66,300,000
Atchison, Topeka & Santa Fe	61,000,000
Kennecott Copper	52,000,000
Total, 8 Corps	$549,900,000
Total, 13 Corps	$1,435,200,000

Again, I think the companies are familiar to every one. The presence of two more railroads in this group (giving the railroads three out of the top fourteen earners) is significant in view of the railroads' present depressed condition and their complaints about the high wages of the railroad workers. Most of the railroads are having a hard time meeting the interest on their bonds in these days, but it was not so long ago that they had ample profits with which some of their bonds might have been paid off. Yet the funded debt of the railroads today is as great as it was in 1929. For during the boom period many railroads were busily engaged in buying up each other's stock at fantastic prices and thus they had little to fall back on when the rainy day arrived.

The profits of the two big copper companies are also interesting in view of the fact that in a subsequent chapter (*Multiple Monopolies*) I have referred to the copper industry as an example of unwarrantably high and uniform prices prevailing in 1929 among the few large producers in this field. The earning power of the automobile business is also beginning to emerge from these figures. For the two petroleum companies (Standard of New Jersey and Standard of Indiana) are to all practical purposes in the auto-accessory business, gasoline being their major product, and a large portion of the Du Pont net came from dividends received through its 23% interest in General Motors.

But we are still more interested in the profits of these companies than in the nature of these companies. Taking the 13 top companies together, we find that they made almost one and one-half billion dollars in 1929. This is over 16% of the net income of all the corporations for that year — about one-sixth of the net income of 456,000 incorporated concerns. It is also 30% of the net income of the 960 Standard Statistic companies — almost one-third of the net income of the companies which we originally isolated as the big-earnings group. If these thirteen companies were included in the 960, as they almost certainly were, we can reduce the 4.7 billion dollar net income of the group to about 3.3 billion dollars by subtracting the net of the top 13 companies. Or, in other words, the 13 companies made over two-fifths as much money as the other 947 of the 960.

There were 55 other companies which in 1929 made more than $20,000,000, but I shall stop at the $40,000,000 mark as far as listing the names and profits of the individual companies is concerned. (But for the $20,000,000 to $40,000,000 companies, see Appendix D, page 277.) There were eight companies which made between $40,000,000 and $50,000,000, namely:

Union Pacific	$49,200,000
Texas Corp	48,300,000
Southern Pacific	47,400,000
Standard of California	46,600,000
Gulf Oil	44,500,000
Bethlehem Steel	42,200,000
Norfolk & Western	41,800,000
Canadian Pacific	41,500,000
Total	$361,500,000
Total, 21 Corps	$1,996,700,000

Those poverty stricken railroads were certainly prosperous enough in 1929, although their names are conspicuously absent from among the big earners of more recent years. We also have three more petroleum companies and only one strictly manufacturing concern. As we shall see, the great difference between the top earners in 1929 and in the 1936-7 "recovery" period is the disappearance of the railroads from the more recent list. But the significance of this change can better be discussed after we have seen the list of big profit makers in the past two years.

Adding the $361,500,000 made by these eight companies to the $1,435,200,000 made by the previous thirteen, we have a total of $1,796,700,000 profits for 21 companies. This amount – close to two billion dollars – is 20.5% of the net income of all corporations – over one-fifth of the national net for 1929. It is also 38% of the net income of the 960 companies in the Standard Statistics list.

The remaining 47 companies making more than $20,000,000 but less than $40,000,000 made a total of $1,298,800,000. This made a grand total for the top 68 companies of $3,095,500,000. The profits of these 68 companies were equal to 35% of the net income of all corporations. They were also equal to 65% of the profits of the 960 Standard Statistics companies.

These figures give us a vivid picture of the highly selective prosperity which prevailed in 1929. It is my conviction, as I have said, that the country as a whole was not prosperous even at that period and that an intense activity was mistaken for a universal prosperity. And the discrepancy between the prosperity and the activity lies precisely in the fact that so much of the profits of business were siphoned off into so few corporate hands. I shall show in the next chapter that a very few thousand big stockholders collected, in the form of dividends, the bulk of the profits made by these companies, that there is no basis for the popular belief that "millions of small stockholders" are the major recipients of the dividends these companies declare. By far the greater portion of their dividends went to large stockholders and served no purpose other than further to enrich already wealthy men. We see, then, that even in the best year of our late boom, the corporations – let alone the people – were not as a group prosperous. For of the total net income of 456,000 companies, more than one-third went to 68 companies making more than $20,000,000 a year. And even if we try to isolate "big business" from business in general, we find that out of 960 major companies, these same 68 made almost two-thirds of all the profits of the whole group.

What happened in 1929 is significant; what happened in 1937 is even more significant, because it is closer to us and because it shows how little the pattern of our industrial life has changed through the depression years. The year 1937 in some respects resembles the year 1929. Both were peak years. Both saw a boom culminate with a crash in the stock market. Both ended in a trough of declining business, great unemployment, and general discouragement. The 1937 prosperity, however, was so much more artificial than even its earlier brother that future historians will hardly consider it even a major interruption to the depression. It was, nonetheless, quite impressive at the time and the Republican Party is now attempting to distinguish between "Depression I" and "Depression II" for the purpose of putting the blame for the second depression on Mr. Roosevelt. As a matter of fact, we had in 1937 not a recovery but an excellent possibility of a recovery – an opportunity lost because the big companies were in too much of a hurry to get back to 1929. For a while, however, the more monopolistic producing companies turned out an excellent imitation of the 1929 article. Notice, however, that the peaks are not as high and the select circle is much smaller. But the top earners made an even greater proportion of all the profits made.

In looking at the 1937 figures we are admittedly handicapped by the fact that our previous point of reference cannot be accurately established; that is, the Government has not yet published a figure for the net income of all corporations for 1937. This net income of all corporations cannot be estimated closely enough to justify the statistical use of the resulting guess. But I have already given my reasons for believing that there must have been a very small net income outside of the $3,226,000,-000 made by the Standard Statistics group.

In 1937 there were 42 companies which made more than $20,000,000. Six made more than $60,000,000, eighteen made between thirty million

and sixty million, and eighteen more made between twenty million and thirty million. The top
six in 1937 were:

General Motors	$196,700,000
American Telephone	182,300,000
Standard of New Jersey	148,000,000
U. S. Steel	94,900,000
E. I. Du Pont de Nemours	88,000,000
General Electric	63,500,000
Total	$773,400,000

The Du Pont company has risen to a place in
the top five, replacing the Pennsylvania Railroad,
and General Electric has moved from 10th position
to 6th. Du Pont and Standard of New Jersey made
more money in 1937 than in 1929. The total profits
of the six companies were equal to 24% of the
total profits of the 960 Standard Statistics companies. Thus 1937 duplicated 1929 with respect
to the concentration of earning power among a
half-dozen top companies which made even the
other select earners look small. And since it is
evident that the net income of all corporations
must have been several billion dollars below the
1929 total, it follows that the leaders in 1937 must
have accounted for a much larger percentage of
the total net income than went to the top companies in 1929 (a percentage which, you remember,
was 10%).

The next earnings group (between 40 and 60 million dollars net for the year) includes nine companies:

Socony-Vacuum................	$56,800,000
Standard of Indiana............	55,900,000
Texas Corp....................	54,600,000
Chrysler.....................	50,700,000
International Nickel............	50,300,000
Kennecott Copper..............	49,800,000
Humble Oil..................	46,900,000
Union Carbide & Carbon.......	42,800,000
Standard of California.........	41,200,000
Total, 9 Corps...........	$449,000,000
Total, 15 Corps..........	$1,222,400,000

As 1929 was a railroad year, so 1937 appears to have been a petroleum year. Socony-Vacuum is a merger of Standard Oil of New York and Vacuum Oil, two pieces of the old Standard Oil Co. which were severed in 1911 but coalesced again in 1931. As separate companies, they had made $75,600,000 in 1929. Of the other oil companies, Texas Corp. and Humble made more money in 1937 than in 1929 and Standard of California made almost as much. The petroleum industry is a bit lacking in the competitive spirit, perhaps because such a large portion of it consists of pieces of Mr. Rockefeller's old "Trust." When the original Standard Oil Company was dissolved in 1911, the dissolution, although making separate corporations out of the various divisions of the old trust, did not disturb the stock ownership. That is, Mr. Rockefeller and his associates held the same percentage of the stocks of the new companies as they had held of the stocks of the old company. It is said that when the news of the dissolution was announced, J. P. Morgan (the elder) remarked, "No law can make a man compete with himself."

It is also true that no law can make a man compete with other men. For several years many oil companies have been operating under agreements as to how much oil each should produce. These agreements, made with the cooperation of State commissions in various oil-producing states, were and are entirely legal. But some of the major oil companies have been also charged with combining to keep up the retail price of gasoline. In January, 1938, a group of 16 large petroleum corporations were convicted of violating the Sherman Anti-Trust Act by raising and fixing gasoline prices. On an appeal to a higher court, however, the conviction was reversed. But no one would argue that anything in the nature of cut-throat competition exists in the petroleum field. The corporate units are too big to battle, too strong to fight.

But what the companies made rather than how they made it still remains the major object of our inquiry. The $449,000,000 made by these nine companies, plus the $773,400,000 made by the previous six companies, gives, for the fifteen companies, a total sum of $1,222,400,000. This is 38%, or almost two-fifths, of the profits made by the 960 Standard Statistics companies. In 1929 the top thirteen companies made about one-third of the profits of the top 960; now we find the top fifteen companies making two-fifths. The highest corporate mountain peaks are still overlooking the rest of the industrial Alps.

I shall list one more group of 1937 earners, those which made more than 30 million but less than 40 million. There were nine companies in this class:

Consolidated Edison	$35,600,000
Chesapeake & Ohio	34,500,000
Woolworth	33,400,000
International Harvester	32,500,000
Gulf Oil	31,800,000
Bethlehem Steel	31,800,000
Norfolk & Western	31,800,000
Anaconda Copper	31,400,000
Sears Roebuck	30,800,000
Total, 9 Corps	$293,600,000
Total, 24 Corps	$1,516,000,000

We have two railroads in this list, but notice that they are not the big general-merchandise lines like the New York Central or the Santa Fe, but specialty railroads, depending chiefly on one commodity – coal. Most of the companies on this list owe their high position to the lowered profits of several big 1929 earners, notably the railroads. The Pennsylvania, for instance, which made $101,400,000 in 1929, dropped to $27,300,000 in 1937. International Harvester, on the other hand, made nearly as much in 1937 as it had made in 1929. There is here a significant point about the 1937 recovery, but I should prefer to note it now and comment on it later.

The profits of these nine companies, plus the profits of the preceding fifteen companies, give, for the twenty-four companies, 1937 earnings of $1,516,000,000. This comes to 47% of the earnings of the 960 Standard Statistics companies. If you will look back at the 1929 tables, you will see that in 1929 the first twenty-one companies made 38% of the earnings of the 960 companies. Year in and year out, some 1,000 companies make the major portion of U. S. profits, and year in and year out, some 20 companies make 40% to 50% of what the 1,000 companies turn in.

The remaining companies which did better than $20,000,000 in 1937 are listed in Appendix E, page 278. There are 18 of them, and they made $438,-500,000. If we add their total to the totals already listed we find that:

In 1937, 42 companies, making more than $20,000,000 each, made $1,954,500,000.

Since the 960 Standard Statistics companies made $3,226,000,000, we also find that:

These 42 companies made 60% of what the 960 leading companies made.

In 1929 companies making more than $20,000,000 made 65% of the profits of the leading 960 companies, but there were then 68 companies in the over-twenty-million-dollar class. If we want to make a more exact comparison with 1929, we should take the first forty-two 1929 companies and see what they did with respect to the leaders for that year. This calculation shows us that the top 42 companies in 1929 made some 52% of what the top 960 companies made in 1929 – again a close parallel to the 1937 situation.

More significant, however, is the 1937 ratio of the profits of the over-twenty-million-dollar companies to the net income of all companies. I do not see how anyone could possibly put the net income of all corporations, even most optimistically, at more than $4,000,000,000 for the year. In fact, I think that figure is extremely high. Yet, giving the net income of all corporations the benefit of the doubt, we see that the $1,954,500,000 made by the top 42 companies is almost 49% of a very generous estimate as to what all corporations may have made. And even the top 68 companies made only 35% of the net income of all corporations in 1929.

Thus we see that the recovery of 1937 was even more selective than the prosperity of 1929.

Before making a final comment on this situation in which so few of the companies habitually make so much of the money, I should like to make a few comparisons between the high earners of 1937 and the high earners of 1929. Suppose, in the first place, we take the earnings of the top 24 companies in 1937 and compare them with the earnings of these same companies in 1929. Remember that these 1937 companies fell into three groups – six companies making more than $60,000,000 (Group A below); nine companies making more than $40,000,000 (Group B below); and nine more companies making more than $30,000,000 (Group C below). The following table shows the 1937 and the 1929 earnings of these groups:

	1937	1929	Ratio, 1937 to 1929
Group A..	$773,000,000	$929,000,000	83%
Group B..	449,000,000	414,000,000	108%
Group C..	294,000,000	402,000,000	73%
Total.....	$1,516,000,000	$1,745,000,000	87%

We see that these 24 companies made, in 1937, 87% as much as they made in 1929. The nine companies in the second group actually made 108% of their

1929 earnings. Of the twenty-four companies, those which made more money in 1937 than in 1929 were (earnings in millions of dollars):

Company	1937	1929
Standard of New Jersey	148	121
E. I. Du Pont de Nemours	88	78
Texas Corp.	54	48
Chrysler	51	22
International Nickel	50	22
Humble Oil	47	32
Union Carbide & Carbon	43	36
Sears, Roebuck	31	30

Other large 1937 earners, not included in the top 24 companies, which made more money in 1937 than in 1929, include (earnings in millions of dollars):

Company	1937	1929
Aluminum Co.	27	25
Procter & Gamble	27	19
Eastman Kodak	22.3	22
Shell Union	20	17
Coca-Cola	25	13

Except for the petroleum companies, we have here 13 companies which, over a considerable period, can operate almost independently of general business conditions (they accounted for 15% of all 1937's estimated profits). Du Pont and Union Carbide and Carbon operate in the chemical industry, a business long famous for the extent to which its leading members avoid stepping on each other's toes. International Nickel produces about 90% of the world's nickel supply, has charged 35 cents a pound for nickel in every year of the past 10 years. Chrysler, of course, is a special case — Mr. Chrysler did not feature the Plymouth in 1929 so the years are not really comparable. Sears, Roebuck has only one other national competitor (Montgomery Ward) in its mail order field. The Aluminum Co. is a 100% monopoly in the producing end of its business. Kodak turns out about 85% of the photographic film made in this country and perhaps 75% of the world supply.

The Coca-Cola company is perhaps the best example of my point. Nobody could accuse the Atlanta soft-drink concern of being an economic or social public enemy and although it has established a trade mark monopoly the establishment has cost it a great many million advertising dollars. And nobody has to drink Coca-Cola unless he wishes to. On the other hand, the Coca-Cola company does earn from 35% to 70% on its capitalization year after year and it obviously can be dizzy with prosperity at a time when the country in general can be going through the most acute phases of the worst depressions. It is almost insulated from the economic conditions of its times.

And so, though not to such a great extent, are these other companies which did so well in 1937 – and most of them turn out products more important than a five-cent drink. In a subsequent chapter (*Multiple Monopolies*), I shall discuss in more detail these companies that keep themselves aloof from the world. At the moment, I should only like to point out the folly of measuring recovery by the restored profits of a few monopolistic companies whose ability to swim is hardly affected by conditions which leave most other companies with a strong tendency to sink.

In this connection, it is significant to remember that the one great profit-making industry of 1929 which showed no signs of coming back was the railroad industry. The New York Central, the Santa Fe, the Union Pacific, the Southern Pacific, and the Canadian Pacific, all big earners in 1929, did not appear in the leading groups in 1937. For the earnings of a railroad reflect, not the prosperity of one company or of one industry, but the prosperity – or at least the *activity* – of all companies and all industries. They reflect it so accurately that their weekly freight car loadings (the amount of freight they ship) is the best single index of the general state of trade. The failure of the railroads to recover an appreciable portion of their 1929 earnings is a measure of the failure of business in general to make a similar recovery. The ability of many 1937 leaders to exceed 1929 profits (and there were many other similar concerns which in 1937 came very close to 1929) is a measure of the extent to which these companies have protected themselves from the ebb and flow (particularly the ebb) of the industrial tide. They are companies which have taken out of society a great deal more than they will ever put back.

All of which brings us back to our major proposition that a few companies make most of the money, and still fewer companies make most of the money that the few companies make. This is not a new proposition. It has been advanced ever since the first industrial consolidations took place. But our parents lost their fear of the "trusts" because a few conspicuous one-company monopolies were "busted" and because of a fatuous distinction between "good trusts" (like U. S. Steel) and "bad trusts" (like the old Standard Oil). We ourselves – or those of us who were old enough to vote in the 1920's – were for the most part inclined to accept the statement that the more money the big companies made, the more money everybody made. We regarded corporations like General Motors and U. S. Steel and American Telephone as so many industrial prophets, leading us into an economic promised land. But since 1929 I should think the bloom must have worn off that particular flower although it is true that in 1937 it was, briefly, again revived.

Today a few companies thrive monopolistically, while the bulk of the companies are in danger of perishing competitively. We are all working for them, whether or not we know it, and the bulk of their profits are going to a few large stockholders, are in no sense being widely divided to serve the general good (of which we shall see more in the next chapter). Some of them are large employers of labor and some are not; but those who do supply large-scale employment are also the first to bring about large-scale unemployment whenever their dividends are threatened. Nothing would be gained and much would be lost by attempting to unscramble the big companies. From the standpoint of useful production, they represent progress which society could not afford to lose. But they do not produce for use; they produce for profit. And they produce for the profit of so few and of such selfish owners that they have become an economic and a social burden which it is becoming constantly more difficult to support.

Chapter III

THE DISTRIBUTION OF DIVIDENDS

A GREAT DEAL of energy has been wasted in attempts to calculate the number of stockholders in American industry. I say wasted energy because, in the first place, there are too many unknown factors in the problem to permit of any solution within a reasonable margin of error. In the second place, *the number of stockholders is not the significant figure.* For even if you could determine or estimate or guess or invent the number of stockholders, you still would not know *how the dividend payments are divided among them.* And this is the important point. Without it, your calculations are going to take some such form as: If *x* equals the number of stockholders and *y* equals the dollars paid out in dividends, then *y* divided by *x* equals the dollars received by each dividend recipient.

We have already seen, in the first chapter, the bad results of such thinking. We have also noticed its prevalence. When times were good, people took the total number of corporations – a known figure –

and the net income of all corporations – also a known figure – divided the second by the first and decided that all the companies were making a little less than $20,000 a year. From any standpoint this conclusion was of course absurd. But if you get a silly answer when you have the advantage of working with two known quantities, you will get a much sillier answer when you try the same problem with one of your quantities indeterminable. It is as if, having failed to do something with two hands, you try to perform a similar feat with one hand tied behind your back.

Thus far I have been discussing this matter only with respect to honest effort and honest error. It has also, however, another aspect. There are speakers and writers (editorial writers, at least) who take the most exaggerated estimates of the number of stockholders, assume that the dividends of all corporations are evenly divided among them, and point the fictitious, usually the mendacious, moral that American industry is owned by the American public. I have seen the statement that the large corporations are owned by, and operated in the interests of, 20,000,000 American citizens. Such statements could be dismissed as merely nonsense except for the fact that they have been made so often that they appear to have won some measure of credence. And from them it is a short step to the proposition that any measure tending to reduce dividend payments would, by injuring these millions upon millions of stockholders (including a remarkable number of widows and orphans with no other means of support) tend to injure the welfare of the people as a whole. The conclusion – and this is the rabbit that the magician has been hiding in the hat – is that there can be no harm in the profits, however high, of the big companies because, after all, who owns the big companies? Why, you and I and all the rest of us – or anyhow, nearly all. The answer to which is that we do nothing of the sort.

Suppose we look at this matter of stockholdings in our so-called "publicly held" companies not from the standpoint of how many persons own one or more shares of stock, but from the standpoint of the manner in which the dividends are divided among whatever number of stockholders there may be. At first sight this approach might appear to be even more difficult than the attempt to count the stockholding noses. And so it is, if we attempt to trace every dividend dollar to its destination. But it is not so difficult to show how most of the dividend dollars are distributed, or to show how few individuals absorb the greater part of dividend returns. I have already referred to the *Statistics of Income*, published by the Bureau of Internal Revenue of the United States Treasury. This invaluable document has two sections "Corporation Returns" and "Individual Returns." As the statistics of corporate income formed the basis for the first chapter of this book, so the statistics of personal income form the basis for the present chapter.

For the Government publication tells not only how much income various classes of income recipients got, but also the sources of the income received. You can find, for instance, how many people got between $5,000 and $10,000 a year in "salaries, wages, commissions, fees, etc." and also the total amount of such wages and salaries received by the persons in this wage-and-salary class. You can get the same information with respect to income from rents, and income from capital gains, and income from various other sources, dividends included. And since (from the corporate income statistics) you can also calculate the total dividends declared by corporations to individuals, you can combine the two sources of information with most decisive results.

Let us look first at 1929 – the year in which the most corporations paid the most dividends and presumably to the most people. In that year, dividends declared to individuals came to $5,750,000,000.* Berle and Means in *The Modern Corporation and Private Property*, estimate that there were from 4,000,000 to 7,000,000 stockholders in 1929. The Twentieth Century Fund has a much more generous estimate of 10,000,000 to 12,000,000 stockholders in 1932. As I have said, it does not much matter how many stockholders there were, but as we are going to see in a moment just how much money some of the stockholders got, we may as well have some point of reference, however vague, to how many stockholders there may have been. Call it 1,000,000 or 20,000,000, if you want to. Or just think of a number.

What we do know, however, and know precisely, is the number of persons in certain dividend-receiving classes and the total amount of dividends they received. The following table shows the first three classes of dividend-recipients according to the Government's *Statistics of Income*, beginning with those persons who received $1,000,000 *in dividends alone* and going down to those who received $250,000 or more *in dividends alone*. Keep in mind

* The corporations declared dividends of $8,350,000,000, but $2,600,000,000 were declared by corporations to other corporations — as by operating companies to holding companies, etc.

that these figures do not represent the total income of these persons, but merely their dividend income:

Dividend Class ($)	No. of Recipients	Dividends Received ($)	% of All Dividends
1,000,000 or more.....	132	271,000,000	4.7
500,000–1,000,000....	267	181,000,000	3.2
250,000 to 500,000....	685	235,000,000	4.0
Total.........1,084		687,000,000	11.9

Here we have exactly 1,084 persons getting exactly 11.9% of all the dividends paid out in 1929. These 1,084 persons therefore owned more than one-tenth of all American industry – or at least the dividend-paying portion thereof. In 1929 the dividend-paying portion of American industry had outstanding about 85 billion dollars in stock, on which it paid 5.6 billion dollars dividends. It therefore required about $15 worth of stock to yield $1 in dividends. In the best-paying section of industry, however, $10 worth of stock yielded $1 in dividends. On this ratio, then, these 1,084 persons, who got $687,000,000 in dividends, must have owned from 10 to 15 times that much stock, or must have owned stock to the value of at least $7,000,000,000 to $10,000,000,000. Think of less than 1100 persons – 1100 individuals – 1100 men, women, widows, and orphans with a 7-to-10 billion-dollar ownership in American industry. That is wealth. That is the concentration of wealth. That is the manner in which American industry is owned today. What does it matter how many stockholders there may be, if so few of them get so much of the dividends? The 1,084 top dividend-getters are, if we take Mr. Berle's most conservative figure of 4,000,000 stockholders, less than three-one-hundredths of one per cent of all stockholders. If we take the editorial writer's favorite figure of 20,000,000 stockholders, the 1,084 are about one two-hundredths of one per cent of all stockholders. Which figure, if either, is correct makes no difference. The point is that 1,084 persons got practically 12% of all the dividends paid out. Remember, too, that 132 out of these 1,084 persons got more than $1,000,000 apiece in dividends alone and collected almost two-fifths of the dividends that the 1,084 got.

Nor does the distribution of dividends get much more even as we go down the list. The next four classes range from those who received just under $250,000 in dividends to those who received $40-000 in dividends:

Dividend Class ($)	No. of Recipients	Dividends Received ($)	% of All Dividends
100,000 to 250,000....	3,484	511,000,000	8.9
75,000 to 100,000.....	2,525	218,000,000	3.8
50,000 to 75,000......	5,545	337,000,000	5.8
40,000 to 50,000......	4,450	199,000,000	3.5
Total..........	16,004	$1,265,000,000	22.0

Here we have 16,004 individuals getting more than a billion and a quarter dollars in dividends – more than one fifth of all the dividends paid out. By our previous reckoning, these 16,004 persons must have had around a 20-billion-dollar stake in American industry. When we combine these 16,004 individuals with our previous 1,084 individuals, we find that a total of 17,088 individuals got dividends totalling $1,952,000,000. *And this amount was 33.9% of all dividends declared.* Think of 17,088 persons collecting nearly two billion dollars in dividends—owning more than one-third of American corporate stock. These are the big stockholders. These are the real investors. These are the capitalists. If there were 4,000,000 stockholders in 1929, these 17,088 individuals were about $\frac{4}{10}$ of one per cent of the group; if there were 20,000,000 stockholders, they were about $\frac{1}{12}$ of one per cent. But they got 34% of the dividends paid.

Remember, too, that stockholders of this size do not own stock in little corporations or middle sized corporations. Small and medium sized companies do not pay the kind of dividends that these people collect. They buy into the big corporations. They center their investments in precisely the small group of heavily capitalized companies which we have discussed in Chapter One as the only portion of American industry that, as a group, consistently makes money year after year. Since these 17,088 persons get one-third of the dividends of industry, it follows that they own one-third of industry. But as their ownership is concentrated in the big companies, they must own very much *more* than one-third of these key concerns.

Let us see if we can find at least an indication of how much of the big companies these people own. In 1929 the 960 companies in the Standard Statistics group made profits of about $4,740,000,000. I do not know how many dollars in dividends these companies paid. But I do know that in 1929 companies of this size and type paid out in dividends approximately 60% of their profits – that is, for every million dollars they made, they paid $600,000 to the stockholders and kept $400,000 for themselves. (Nowadays the dividends are usually a higher percentage of the profit, but that is because the companies are trying to make up for dividends passed in earlier years of the depression, with perhaps assistance from the late undistributed profits tax.) If the 960 companies paid 60% of their 1929 profits in dividends, their dividend payments for that year came to approximately $2,840,000,000. So $2,840,000,000 represents the amount that all the stockholders owning all the stock in these 960 companies got. We have already seen, however, that these 17,088 individuals got dividends of $1,950,000,000. This amount is 69% of the amount of dividends declared by the 960 companies. It therefore follows that the stockholdings of these 17,088 persons are equivalent to a 69% ownership of the 960 companies which dominate the industrial scene. It is not a question of these persons owning *one*-third of all industry. It is a question of their owning well over *two*-thirds of *profitable* industry, of the big money makers, the big dividend payers, of the very companies whose profits are supposedly socially justifiable because so many millions of stockholders share in their dividends.

The next group of dividend recipients brings us down to those who received dividends of only $20,000 a year:

Dividend Class ($)	No. of Recipients	Dividends Received ($)	% of All Dividends
30,000 to 40,000.....	7,584	261,000,000	4.5
25,000 to 30,000.....	6,109	166,000,000	2.9
20,000 to 25,000.....	8,111	183,000,000	3.2
Totals.........	21,804	610,000,000	10.6

Here we have another one tenth of all the dividends declared going to a group of 21,804 persons – and remember that a man with a dividend income of even $20,000 a year may have a total income of some $100,000 a year, since dividends account for hardly more than 20% of income in this bracket.

If we add these 21,804 persons to the 17,088 in

the previous groups, we have 38,892 persons whose 1929 dividend payments came to $20,000 a year or more. The dividends received by these 38,892 persons totalled $2,562,000,000. This amount is over 44% of all the dividends paid in 1929. Less than 40,000 stockholders got dividends of more than two and one-half billion dollars. On a basis of 4,000,000 stockholders, these persons were a little less than 1% of all stockholders; on a basis of 20,000,000, they were about $\frac{1}{5}$ of one per cent. On any basis, they got more than $2 out of every $5 paid.

I have been discussing what dividends of this size mean in terms of total stockholdings and of ownership in industry. Perhaps a better way to grasp the scale of these payments is to compare them with some other forms of payments in 1929.

There were, in that year, 8,800,000 wage earners in manufacturing industries. These men and women were paid a total wage for the year of $11,600,000,000. (Their average wage was $1320 a year.) The dividends paid to the 38,892 high dividend getters were equal to more than one-fifth of the wages paid to the 8,800,000 wage-earners in manufacturing.

There were also, in 1929, about 4,500,000 persons employed in retail trade. Their wages came to $5,200,000,000 (about $1180 a year). The dividends paid to the 38,892 high dividend getters were equal to one half the wages of the 4,500,000 persons employed in retail trade.

There were, in 1929, about 6,300,000 farmers. The cash income from farm production for that year was $10,400,000,000. The dividends paid to the 38,892 high dividend receivers equalled 24.6% (approximately one-fourth) of the cash value of 6,300,000 farmers' products.

The 1929 total of all wage earners and salary earners and the total national payroll are matters of estimate, but most estimates agree closely with the U. S. Department of Commerce figures of 35,000,000 jobholders and a national payroll of $51,000,000,000. On this basis, the dividends of the 38,892 high dividend getters were 5% of the national payroll.

The remainder of the dividends were more widely distributed, but as the distribution widens the dividends per recipient rapidly decline. The next table shows dividend recipients in the $5,000 to $20,000 a year classes.

Dividend Class ($)	No. of Recipients	Dividends Received ($)	% of All Dividends
15,000 to 20,000..	14,905	257,000,000	4.5
10,000 to 15,000..	30,278	365,000,000	6.3
5,000 to 10,000...	71,592	491,000,000	8.5
Totals......	116,775	1,113,000,000	19.3

These 116,775 persons received a little less in dividends than was received by about 4,500 persons whose dividends were $100,000 apiece or more. Grouping them with our previous 38,892 high dividend recipients, we have 155,667 dividend getters, with $3,675,000,000 in dividends received. This amount is 64% of all dividends paid in 1929. If there were 4,000,000 stockholders, these 155,667 persons were less than 4% of the total; if there were 20,000,000 stockholders, this group was less than one per cent of the total. In any case, the 155,667 got $6.40 out of every $10 paid.

The remaining dividend classes listed in the Government figures bring us down to the small stockholder of whom we have heard so much and who undoubtedly exists in very considerable numbers. The final classes were:

Dividend Class ($)	No. of Recipients	Dividends Received ($)	% of All Dividends
1,000 to 5,000	196,645	485,000,000	8.4
Less than 1,000	244,691	86,400,000	1.5
Totals	441,336	571,400,000	9.9

These are really two separate categories, for the less-than-$1,000 group can, and does, trail off almost to nothing. The 196,645 persons in the $1,000 to $5,000 class represent, for the most part, well to do, upper middle class people with a substantial dividend income (about $2500 apiece). It is difficult to generalize about the 244,691 persons who received less than $1,000, since this class ranges from proprietors and officers of medium sized businesses to salary earners with a few shares of the company's stock. The average dividend in this group was $350 per person. But there were 57,000 of its 244,700 members whose dividends were not only less than $1,000 but also less than $100, and whose average dividend was $46. The most significant point about the 244,000 is that this group, by far the largest of the various classes, received 1.5% of all the dividends paid.

The *Statistics of Income* supplies detailed information only on the dividends received by persons with a net income of $5,000 a year or more. It therefore accounts for only about 600,000 dividend recipients who, however, received a little less than 74% of all dividends paid.* There is no way of determining where the rest of the dividends went, although (see footnote) nearly a billion dollars was reported by persons filing reports with no net incomes or incomes of less than $5,000 for the year. Inasmuch as a good many persons with

---

* The Government also reported $540,000,000 in dividends received by persons whose net income was less than $5,000 a year. There were 3,000,000 persons in this category, but the Government does not say how many of them received dividends. The Government also reported $300,-000,000 of dividends that went to persons with no net income — that is, to those whose legal deductions were greater than their income received. This leaves about $700,000,000 in dividends received by persons who did not file a Federal income tax for 1929.

high total incomes listed deductions large enough to bring their net taxable income down to less than $5,000, it is not possible to divide this class into the poor but honest and the not so poor but not so honest. The significant point is still the fact that, to no matter how many millions of persons the remainder of the dividend money may have gone, it must have amounted to very little per person. You will remember that there were 57,000 persons in the over-$5,000-a-year net income class whose dividends were less than $100 each and averaged $46. Since the persons reporting less than $5,000 net income, or reporting no net income, or not filing Federal tax returns at all, must have been, as a group, less prosperous than the Federal taxpayers, they should have received, as individuals, even less than the $46 average in the lowest tax-paying group.

As for dividend payments in years subsequent to 1929, although total payments are lower, the pattern of their distribution repeats itself with extraordinarily little change. In 1932, for example, dividends paid to individuals totalled $2,625,000-000. In that year there were 315 individuals whose dividends came to more than $250,000 each, and whose total dividends came to about $190,000,000, which was 7% of all dividends paid. In the same year, there were 20,817 persons (including the

315 mentioned above) whose dividends totalled $956,000,000, which was 36% of all dividends paid (and if there were 12,000,000 stockholders that year, these 20,500 persons came to less than $\frac{2}{10}$ of one per cent of them). In 1929, you will remember, the top 17,000 dividend getters got 34% of the dividends. So in both years the share of the few top dividend recipients was about the same. And in 1934, when individual dividend payments had risen to $2,760,000,000, we find 21,554 individuals collecting $975,800,000, which again is 35% of all the dividends declared.

Year in and year out, in good times and in bad, the Government figures show that about 1,000 of the largest stockholders collect about 10% of the dividends; that about 20,000 large stockholders collect over one-third of the dividends; that about 40,000 large stockholders collect about two-fifths of the dividends. It is, therefore, hardly more than an idle speculation to debate the number of stockholders. For it is the big stockholders who get the big dividends, the big stockholders whose big stockholdings are concentrated in the big companies that make the big profits. Remember that in 1929 (and in other years as well, for the very large stockholder usually maintains at least a life-interest in the corporations whose securities he holds in such large quantities) the dividends received by 17,088 persons were equal to 69% of the dividends paid by the 960 companies which made half of the net income of all corporations for that year. This is the most significant of the points shown by our analysis of the distribution of dividends.

It should also be evident, even aside from the statistical proof, that if there are four or seven or ten or twelve million stockholders in American corporations, most of them must have very minute quantities of stock. For where does anyone think that all these millions of persons got the money to buy any appreciable quantity of stock with? Even in 1929, according to the Brookings Institution,* there were less than 6,000,000 families (out of 27,500,000) with incomes of more than $3,000 a year and only 2,250,000 families with incomes of more than $5,000 a year. Most of America's 27-500,000 families put their savings, if any, in a bank. And certainly the family income has not improved since 1929, although it was as of 1932 that the Twentieth Century Fund made its estimate of 10,000,000 to 12,000,000 stockholders – a year in which the national income was less than half of

* In *America's Capacity to Consume.*

what it had been in 1929. At first sight it seems incredible that there should be even 4,000,000 stockholders, let alone 12,000,000. But there are undoubtedly a good many more stockholders than any study of individual or family incomes would indicate.

For certain very large corporations have gone to great pains to distribute their stock to the public (and also, in some cases, to their employees). These companies are chiefly, although not entirely, in the public utility field. Over a long period of years they have carried on a drive for "customer ownership" – that is, they have conducted campaigns of stock-selling to their customers with the avowed purpose of creating public goodwill. The late Samuel Insull was a great advocate of this technique, and hundreds of electric light and power companies throughout the country have followed his example in selling a very small portion of their shares in minute lots to as many of their customers as could be persuaded to buy them.

The American Telephone and Telegraph Co. is, however, probably the largest-scale practitioner of stock-selling to customers. (After all, it has 15,300,000 customers to sell to.) It organized for this purpose a special company (Bell Securities Co.) headed by Arthur Page, a vice-president of the parent concern. Mr. Page and his stock-salesmen did an excellent job selling American Telephone stock to telephone users. Indeed, the company has some 640,000 stockholders on its books today. And – as I cannot remember when the Telephone Co. has failed to pay a dividend – we have some 640,000 dividend recipients in this one company alone. (American Telephone stockholders would account for a little less than one-sixth of all stockholders, on Mr. Berle's 4,000,000 stockholder estimate.) But how foolish it would be to conclude that the run-of-mine customer-stockholder "owns" American Telephone, let alone American industry as a whole. American Telephone stock pays a $9 dividend per share; during the boom period it was selling at from around $150 to $310 a share; and it is one of the few stocks that has remained at well over $100 a share for the major part of the depression period. It seems unlikely that many of Mr. Page's customer-stockholders could afford to buy enough Telephone stock to make their dividends any significant portion of their incomes or to become investors in any real sense. And indeed, in 1929, the company's own report stated that over 37% of its stockholders (then numbering 470,000) owned *5 shares or less* of its stock; and over 57% of them owned *10 shares or less.*

What I have been saying is not a criticism of American Telephone. I have met (briefly and pro-

fessionally) several hundred major corporate executives during the past ten years, and I should
certainly come very close to putting Mr. Page at
the top of the list. His customers got what is probably the best investment in American industry
since very few securities pay a $9 dividend and
never pass it. Also Mr. Page stopped selling
American Telephone stock when stock market
speculation ran the price up beyond its reasonable
value. Nor can the company be criticized for creating customer goodwill by making its customers
owners of its stock. Nevertheless, American Telephone's 640,000 stockholders, numerically impressive though they may be, show how dangerous it is
to judge the "ownership" of American industry
from the number of persons who are technically
part-owners of it. And remember that this company is only one of the many public utilities with
similar customer-stockholder plans.

Employee-stockholder plans also produce large
numbers of stockholders with extremely insignifi-
cant holdings. A good many of these plans were
initiated during the later stages of the 1920's, when
the corporations were making plenty of money and
feeling well disposed toward their hired hands. It
was, however, an unfortunate time to embark
upon employee ownership campaigns, for although
the corporations were acting in all good faith, they

frequently sold the shares at bull market prices which did not long prevail. When the depression arrived, the value of the stock often dropped far below what the employees had paid (or were paying, on the installment plan) for it, and it was also unfortunately necessary to fire a considerable number of the recently created "owners" of the concern. There is no more ironic comment upon the boom-time paternalism which industry sometimes exhibited during the 1920's than the situation of a man who, with maybe another six months' payments to make on half a dozen shares of the company's stock, discovered that just as he was on the eve of becoming a little partner in the concern, one of the big partners had fired him. Even the plans that survived the depression have not resulted in any appreciable degree of employee-ownership. I have seen the number of employee-stockholders in American industry estimated at more than a million. But here again we have a large number of owners with a microscopic degree of ownership.

A much more characteristic division of stockholders and stockholdings is seen in the E. I. Du Pont de Nemours company. The big chemical concern has only about 56,000 common stockholders; even if its dividends ($69,000,000 in 1937) were equally divided among the 56,000 it could hardly be considered "publicly-owned." But their division is far from equal. The Du Pont company has outstanding about 11,000,000 shares of common stock. The largest stockholder in the corporation is another corporation, the Christiana Securities Co. This company is a private holding company of the Du Pont clique. Of its seven directors, four are Du Ponts, including Pierre S., the present head of the clan. A fifth is John J. Raskob, who may be considered a Du Pont by adoption. The business of the Christiana Securities Co. is to hold large blocks of securities for the Du Ponts and their immediate friends and associates. Its chief assets are 3,000,000 shares (27%) of Du Pont common. Now here, technically, is one stockholder. But he — or rather it — owns 3,000,000 shares. And when the Du Pont company declared its 1937 common dividend of $69,000,000, $19,000,000 of this amount went straight into the family holding company's hands. Here is, of course, the other extreme of ownership — in most of the large corporations the leading stockholder is not quite so far ahead of the pack. Nevertheless, when you think about the ownership of American industry, remember that one stockholder may have one share or one million shares. And the consequent difference in the degree of ownership is extremely marked.

The myth about the "publicly held" corporations "owned" by the public is perhaps the least well founded and also the most harmful of the many illusions commonly prevailing about American corporate life. Even the expression "publicly held" is a misnomer. It suggests that because a corporation may offer its stock to the public, the public in general acquires a significant degree of ownership in it. It might as well be argued that because art museums are open to the public, everybody can take home a Rembrandt.

There is a close analogy between the distribution of dividends and the distribution of profits. We saw in the first chapter the extent to which a group of less than a thousand companies have monopolized the profits of American trade, although some 475,000 corporations are doing business in this country today. We have seen in this chapter how invariably around 20,000 big stockholders, some of whom collect annual dividends of $1,000,000 or more,* collect more than one-third of all the dividends. We have also seen that these few large investors (never as much as one per cent of all stockholders) own far more than the equivalent of one-third of the large corporations, because it is in

* Even in 1932 there were 27 dividend collectors in the million-dollars-a-year dividend class.

these corporations alone that almost their entire investment is made. These same few persons, getting dividends by the billions of dollars per year, employ their dividend money to buy more stock with which to get more dividends, and so on without end. So, again the next time that you hear somebody talking about how many people own American industry, ask him how many people own how much.

Chapter IV

MULTIPLE MONOPOLY

THE CONFLICT between the few corporations that always make money and the many corporations that usually report deficits is often thought of as a conflict between Big Business and Little Business. There is a great deal of truth in this concept. All the companies with consistently large profits are big companies. And, generally speaking, the smaller the company, the less chance it has to show a profit for the year. Yet an explanation of profits or losses in terms entirely of size is subject to many exceptions. It is an oversimplification, for it attempts to explain a many-sided situation in terms of only one of its factors.

For instance, not all big companies make money. The American Woolen Co., by far the largest textile corporation, has been a consistent loser since 1927. The International Mercantile Marine Co., organized by the elder J. P. Morgan in an attempt to consolidate the shipping industry as he had already consolidated the steel industry, was as great a failure as the U. S. Steel Corporation eventually was a success. There are also many relatively small companies which show a very high profit in comparison to the money invested in them. It must also be remembered that in speaking of incorporated business only we are ruling out most of the one-man or family companies which do not bother to take out incorporation papers.

To set up Big Business as opposed to Little Business also ignores the point that the little business man nearly always identifies himself with the big business man. In February, 1938, the small business men held a convention in Washington. The sessions degenerated into disorder and low comedy; the chief ambition of the delegates appeared to be a desire to see the President; and a group of business men who could be considered small only in comparison with General Motors or American Telephone appeared to take a very important part in the decisions which the convention made. But, even with allowance for this influence, the attitude of small business was more openly reactionary than the attitude of big business.

It was these little business men who came out flatly for the repeal of the Social Security Act. The taxes imposed under this act are hated by big business at least as much as by little business.

But the large industrialist and the capitalist have not yet become bold enough to make a direct attack on them. Big business knows that the Social Security Act represented a protest, however limited, against the insecurity of the jobholder and the growing "obsolescence" of the worker who has passed the 40-year mark. It moves cautiously, therefore, afraid to arouse public opinion over an issue on which its position cannot be defended. But the little business men had no such inhibitions. They denounced social security without the slightest hesitation. If big business was waiting to see what the reaction of the public would be to this gesture, big business must have been disappointed. For the serious aspects of the small business men's convention were so overshadowed by its comic aspects that even reactionary newspapers could not report the proceedings with a straight face.

Thus it remains essential to avoid looking at big business as the dragon and little business as the Saint George. For in this instance the Saint does not know any better than to be on the same side as the dragon. The small business man is even more likely to overwork and underpay his labor; he is at least as bitter in his resentment toward labor unions; and we have already seen that his opposition to taxes is even more openly expressed. He has, however, a better excuse for his attitude, although it remains an anti-social attitude none the less. The small business man often does scrape along with a very small profit margin which may at any moment disappear. To him a union shop and a wage increase might mean that he could no longer stay in business, whereas to his big brother better pay to organized workers is feared and hated almost solely because it might interfere with dividend payments. As for taxes, it is indeed stupid to tax one man as much as 14% of a $20,000 corporate income and another man as little as $16\frac{1}{2}\%$ of a $20,000,000 corporate income. Yet the little business man is partly responsible for this situation. If he insists upon standing shoulder to shoulder with Tom Girdler and James Rand he cannot expect Congress to recognize the fact that the welfare of the Anaconda Copper Mining Company and the welfare of the corner druggist are by no means fostered by the same measures.

The essential difference between the corporate money makers and the corporate money losers is the difference between operating on a monopoly basis and operating on a competitive basis. In more general terms, we may say that in this country we have two forms of capitalism — monopoly capitalism and competitive capitalism. They operate side by side; the monopoly capitalist has no animus toward the competitive capitalist:

and both are in business with the object of making as much money as circumstances will permit. But the monopoly capitalist exercises a very strong influence over the circumstances, whereas the competitive capitalist is the victim of his environment. Few companies are strong enough to operate monopolistically, yet profits in American industry are almost in direct proportion to the extent to which competitition has been eliminated. A numerically overwhelming number of all corporations do business today in fields where competition is still both free and fierce. But these are not the companies that make the choice profits and pay the choice dividends. They are the companies wh.ch make small profits in good times and sustain consistent deficits in bad times. Business in this country has become a question of the survival of the least competitive.

The fact that most corporations do operate competitively and that nearly all corporations with which the public comes into direct contact belong to this category has made it difficult for the public to get a clear picture of the situation. No matter how monopolistic a corporation may be, it always pretends to be the most competitive concern that ever squeezed a penny's profit out of a dollar's sales. The same concerns which have done the most to take the individuality out of enterprise and remove the risk from investment are the loudest in their appeals to the "American way," to "rugged individualism," to the very competitive system which in their own industries they have either eliminated or largely removed. They always pose as poor boys trying to get along; and because most of the business men whom you and I may personally know are comparatively poor boys not getting along very well, the impersonation is often successful.

The greatest difficulty in detecting monopolies comes from the fact that even the most monopolistic industry usually contains at least two, and often a dozen or more, very large corporations which make an elaborate pretence of competing with each other. The public is accustomed to think of "pure" monopolies – of companies which have no competition whatsoever. Electric light and power companies are local monopolies. Railroads, to a very considerable extent, are regional monopolies. American Telephone, despite a few scattered "independent companies" is essentially a monopoly on a national scale. But these monopolies are recognized and regulated as such. Their rates may be too high. Their capitalization may be excessive. Their profits may be too great. But at least they do not claim to be competitive concerns. They are not exponents of individualism, rugged or otherwise. They cannot fix prices to suit themselves and, although they may not be sufficiently regulated, the machinery for regulating them exists and the necessity for regulation is admitted. The outright monopoly is not nearly so much a menace to society as the monopolistic company which hides its true character under a competitive disguise.

The distinguishing characteristic of a monopolized industry is that, although it may have more than one large corporate member, it does not have many large corporate members. There are only two large sulphur companies, three large copper companies, four large cigarette companies, hardly a dozen large steel companies, and so on. These companies are not regulated. No outsider dictates their prices. They pose as exponents of individual enterprise and free competition. They are not the products of individual enterprise — they are the products of pooled capital. They cherish each other's profits almost as dearly as they cherish their own. And competition, particularly price competition, is to them an abhorrent term. But whenever they are accused of being monopolies they can always cite the presence of a competitor in the same field. The public does not yet realize that the so-called competitor does not necessarily compete. I suppose it imagines that "standard priced" cigarettes always sell for close to 15 cents a pack, regardless of the cost of the tobacco that goes into them, merely through a coincidence. Even the antitrust laws are based on the principle that a company cannot be considered a "trust" unless its methods of doing business have made the existence of competitive companies difficult or impossible.

This kind of thinking is out of date. The monopoly of today is industrial rather than corporate. It represents a combination of companies who have a cooperative rather than a competitive point of view. The modern monopoly does not acquire its position by eliminating *competitors*. It acquires its position by eliminating *competition*. It does not eliminate *all* competition. Even monopolistic companies compete with each other for customers and in a broad sense all industries are in competition for the consumer's dollar. Competition of this sort, however, serves only to inflate periods of prosperity and prolong periods of depression. The only effective form of competition, particularly from the standpoint of the customer, is *price competition among producers*. The whole theory of orthodox capitalism is based on the concept that every producer will sell at a price as close as possible to his costs, for, if he permits the spread between costs and selling price to broaden, some other producer with a narrower profit margin will take away his market by selling the same product at a lower price. Every orthodox economist, from Adam Smith (who wrote *The Wealth of Nations* in 1775) to the textbook writer of today, assumes that price competition between producers in the same business must be the determining factor in the selling price of all commodities. Otherwise the public would have no protection from high prices and a condition of actual, if not nominal, monopoly would exist.

But modern industry — particularly large scale, mass production industry that does not sell directly to the ultimate consumer — does not believe in competition of this sort. In the place of price competition it has substituted what it calls a *price structure*. Instead of competitive prices, it has established what it calls *stabilized prices*, but which would more honestly be known as *fixed* prices. In the copper industry, the steel industry, the glass industry, the can industry, the industrial chemical industry, the electrical and farm equipment industries, the machinery industry, the cigarette industry (and in nearly every basic producing industry in the United States) the producer thinks of his profits before he thinks of his costs. Even in a depression period, when the producer is unable to sell more than a fraction of his output at "prosperity" prices, he prefers to stick to his price structure and take his losses, if necessary, through large reductions in sales.

In the summer of 1932, for example, the steel industry was operating at below 14% of its capacity. Almost seven-eighths of its plant was standing idle – and so were more than half of its workers. Yet the industry had fought so stubbornly, and so successfully, to maintain its prices that from 1929 to 1932 average steel prices had dropped less than 25%. More completely ironclad monopolies, like the International Nickel Company and the Aluminum Company, paid even less attention to the depression in so far as it affected their prices. Aluminum sold for 24 cents a pound in 1929 and for 23 cents a pound in 1932. Nickel has never budged from its 35 cents a pound price since 1929. These two examples do not illustrate price-fixing, however, since the Aluminum Co. has no (U. S.) competitor in the production of aluminum and International Nickel has no sizeable competitor in the production of nickel. But they do illustrate the price policy of monopolistic concerns: let sales go down, let employment go down, let everything else go down, but keep the prices up. On the other hand, a commodity sold in a truly competitive market – the farmer's crops are a good example – always sacrifices prices to sales. Corn, for instance, sold at an average price of 94 cents a bushel in 1929. In 1932 the number of bushels sold was some 10% greater than in the boom year. *But the farmer got 31 cents a bushel for his corn that year.* In a similarly competitive market, steel prices would follow the same course. The fact that the metal price has an entirely different pattern is evidence of industrial monopoly — an inter-corporate policy of high fixed prices stuck to through thick and thin.

The big producer does not much mind being called an economic royalist, a reactionary, a Tory, or a Fascist. He does not consider himself any of these things; but even if he thought he were all of them — and was fully aware of their implications — he would still find himself in what he would consider very good company indeed. If you really want to make him lose his temper, call him a price cutter.* But be careful when you do it, for remember that those are fighting words.

Many people still believe that competition is the guiding principle of American economic life,

---

* There were whispers that Ernest Weir of National Steel was a price cutter in the days before Mr. Weir's distinguished service in the labor-fighting cause, but I have never found any proof that this canard was based on anything but calumny and spite.

and the concept of competition is deeply rooted in orthodox economic thought. Indeed, the professorial economist, remote in the seclusion of the campus, still tends to deceive the young and delude the ignorant by contending that the "laws" of competitive capitalism make industrial monopolies impossible.

It is not necessary to consider at any length the argument that price fixing does not exist because it is illegal. Producers almost certainly do not enter into written agreements about prices, not because such agreements are illegal but because they are superfluous. Even the so-called "gentlemen's agreements" among them do not necessarily imply clasped hands across the table or verbal bargains made in the dark of the moon. The biggest company may take the initiative in the matter of establishing a price, but the other companies follow not through compulsion but through choice. Unless our anti-trust laws are so radically amended that price uniformity among various producers is considered in itself evidence of collusion, a price can be as fixed as the North Star without either a written document or a verbal understanding to hold it in place.

Somewhat more worthy of consideration, however, is the argument that although prices may *be* fixed they cannot *stay* fixed. For, according to the classic economic theory, the profits in a price-fixed industry would be so great that new competitors would enter the field and sell below the fixed price for the sake of getting themselves a foothold in their new market. A variation of this proposition is seen in the argument that a well organized, well managed, low-cost producer will keep prices close to costs to expand his sales and that the high-cost producer must meet the low-cost price in order to stay in business at all.

These arguments seem to be very logical and they unquestionably apply to businesses which can be entered without making a large initial investment. But remember that there is no such thing as a "little" copper mine or a "little" auto company or a "little" steel mill. If you had a million dollars you could become a large unit in the retail shoe industry but if you put a million dollars into copper you would emerge not even with a small mine, but merely with a big hole. When you get into types of enterprise that require millions of dollars to begin and more millions to operate, you are getting beyond the limits of individual capital and into the sphere of pooled capital. And in this field the spirit of competition is lacking. The will to compete does not exist. Capitalists talk a great deal about the risks of enterprise. But even before they enter the enterprise they do everything possible to see that the risks are minimized. They are like the crooked gambler who, arrested for operating a game of chance, maintained that no conviction was possible because in his game the element of chance had been almost entirely removed.

Suppose we look at the sulphur industry as an example of competition's decline. The sulphur business does not get much into the newspapers because you and I do not buy sulphur. Neither do we buy the sulphuric acid in the manufacture of which most of the sulphur mined throughout the world is used. But sulphur is a basic raw material, for sulphuric acid is so widely used in industry that a good index of the industrial progress of any country is the amount of sulphuric acid consumed within its borders.

There are only two large-scale producers of sulphur in the United States. They are the Texas Gulf Sulphur Co. and the Freeport Sulphur Co.* Larger of the two is Texas Gulf, which has about twice the annual output of Freeport. Both companies work large sulphur deposits in Texas, in the midst of the Texas oil-fields. Texas Gulf originally leased its properties from Gulf Oil (the Mellon petroleum company), its sulphur having been discovered by prospectors who were looking for oil.

* Formerly the Freeport-Texas Co. The name was changed in 1936.

Gulf Oil still has about a one-third interest in Texas Gulf. The Freeport deposits were also originally acquired in the hope that the acreage might contain petroleum. As things turned out, however, the sulphur was an even more valuable discovery. For whereas various sections of the earth's surface in Texas, Oklahoma, California, and other petroleum producing states will, if properly punctured, gush petroleum, the only places so far discovered anywhere in the world where almost pure sulphur lies barely beneath the earth's surface lie in the relatively few square miles which Texas Gulf and Freeport work.

There is, to be sure, plenty of sulphur in the earth's makeup and a sulphur industry existed long before the Texas and Freeport deposits were explored. But sulphur is usually found in combination with iron in the form of iron pyrites, which have to be roasted before the pure sulphur can be extracted from them. The Texas companies do not possess a monopoly of sulphur, but they do possess a near-monopoly of low-cost sulphur. A freak of nature has presented them with apparently inexhaustible supplies of pure sulphur available at the very minimum of mining costs.

Yet neither company attempted to sell its sulphur on any reasonable cost-plus basis, nor did either company attempt to upset the other's profits by cutting the other's price. As long ago as 1926 both companies were selling sulphur at $18 a ton — and ever since 1926 sulphur has stayed at $18 a ton in good times and in bad. For twelve years the "price structure" in sulphur has been so well "stabilized" that no fluctuation has taken place. Yet this period covered the worst years of the depression, years in which the consumption of sulphur experienced a marked decline. According to the "law" of supply and demand, the price of sulphur should have fallen in accordance with the reduced demand for it. But this law, like many other economic concepts still credited with a force which they no longer possess, is subject to monopoly repeal. The sulphur companies sold less sulphur in 1932 than they had sold in 1929. But what they sold, they sold at 1929 prices. And they are selling sulphur at 1929 prices today.

As a result of low costs and high profits, the Texas Gulf company makes $1.00 profit for every $2.00 of sales. Over a ten year period (1926–35) its sales of sulphur totalled $206,000,000. *Its net income on these sales was $103,000,000.* I know of no other company, operating with a comparable sales volume, which shows such a ratio of profit to sales. In most businesses a 10% net to gross is high; 20% is rare indeed. (In the retail field, a profit of 2½ cents per dollar sale is considered good.) For a company producing a fundamental industrial necessity on a large scale to net 50% of its gross over a period including the worst years American industry has ever seen is, I think, an unparallelled record. It is unquestionably an outstanding example of monopoly pricing. The smaller section of the sulphur monopoly (the Freeport company) has not done so well. It expanded into the production of other metals, and it pays 70% of the profits realized from one its sulphur deposits to The Texas Co., the petroleum company from which this acreage is leased. Even with these handicaps, however, Freeport managed to turn 23% of its 1926-35 gross income into net profit.

It is obvious that the position, the prices, and the profits of a company such as Texas Gulf cannot possibly be made to fit into any competitive scheme. The competitive theory is based on the survival of the fittest. Through a freak of nature, the Texas Gulf company was undoubtedly the most fit. Instead of getting $18 a ton for its sulphur, it could have sold sulphur for $16 a ton and made a very large profit. It could have sold at $14 a ton and still done very well indeed. At anything over $10 a ton it would have earned enough money to have given its investors the "fair" return on their investment that investors talk about so much. It does not make much sense to argue about whether Texas Gulf *should* have sold its sulphur at a price closer to its costs. The point is that it certainly should have *according to the competitive theory* and it equally certainly did not.

The immediate victim of its high-price policy was the industrial chemist — the manufacturer of sulphuric acid. As the chemical industry (headed by E. I. Du Pont de Nemours & Co.) is nearly as well organized as the sulphur business, no one need fell sorry for the sulphur buyers. Indeed, the manufacturer of sulphuric acid merely passed the high cost of sulphur along in the form of correspondingly high-priced sulphuric acid. For during the same years that sulphur has always sold for $18 a ton, sulphuric acid has always sold for 78 cents a pound. The fixed price of the sulphur has been duplicated by the fixed price of the acid. There are few better examples of price "stability" extending along the industrial line from basic producer to final seller, with the ultimate consumer finally cracking under the strain.

But though the policies of the sulphur companies cannot be explained with reference to any philosophy of competition, they require no explanation in view of the monopolistic nature of the two concerns. The dollars behind Texas Gulf are not hostile to the dollars behind Freeport; one dollar hardly ever fights with another dollar because experience has shown that in the event of a conflict both dollars get hurt. I do not for a moment imagine that any price-fixing agreement exists between the two corporations. Perhaps the "rival" sales managers do not speak to each other when they meet. Possibly one of the corporations has hired an advertising agency to claim that its sulphur is more sulphuric than the other's. Yet it is foolish to argue that the two companies illustrate the workings of the competitive system. They illustrate perfectly the workings of the monopolistic system — and the same illustration is presented by every industry which is susceptible to the monopolization technique.

The copper industry is another excellent example of a business in which prices are based on how much the customer will stand for, not on how little it may cost to produce the product. Unlike the sulphur industry, the copper industry exhibits no element of "natural" monopoly. Copper mines are scattered throughout the United States and for that matter throughout the world. The three largest North American producers, however, (Kennecott, Anaconda, and Phelps Dodge) turn out about 80% of the total U. S. production, and the copper industry has a trade association to which most of the important producers belong.

It is not possible to say what copper costs to produce, since the costs are different at every mine. A majority of operators, however, can show a profit with copper at 9 cents a pound (the price fixed by the N.R.A. in 1934) and 10-cent copper should be profitable to all but the distinctly high-cost producers. In a system of freely moving prices, copper would presumably not stray far from the 10-cent figure, as any producer charging much above that level would theoretically be undersold by his competitors and unable to find a customer.

But the copper producers do not seem to have read Adam Smith or indeed to be very well acquainted with the competitive idea. In 1928, for example, copper was selling at 15 cents a pound — a boom-time price all out of line with production costs. Early in 1929, however, a series of price increases raised the price of copper to 24 cents a pound, a really fantastic figure never before approached except during the War. There was no corresponding increase in the cost of production. Neither was there any C.I.O. or any New Deal taxes on which to blame the boost. The price went up because the copper producer decided that his customers would stand for it. Most of his customers were making large profits and one very large customer, the auto maker, was making remarkably large profits indeed. So the copper man marked up his copper for the simple reason that he figured he could get away with it. And, for the time being, he was quite correct. In October, to be sure, prosperity, loaded down with the burden of almost universal price increases, collapsed and copper's price structure collapsed soon after. But while the sun had been shining, the copper companies had made plenty of hay.

During the 1937 boom period the copper companies gave a conclusive demonstration of their inability to learn by experience. In October, 1936, copper was selling at 10 cents a pound. But a recovery spirit was in the air and the copper industry was one of the several large basic producers to decide that 1929 was again with us and to act on that delusion. During the next five months the price of copper moved steadily upward until in March, 1937, it reached a peak of 16 cents a pound. This was a 60% increase, as great an increase as would have been made in the food industry if a five-cent cup of coffee had been marked up to eight cents or a ten-cent loaf of bread to sixteen cents. There were no corresponding increases in the cost of producing copper. No new taxes had been suddenly levied; no big strikes hastily called. The guiding principle, as in 1929, was what the traffic would bear. This is the only principle on which monopoly prices are ever based. The 1937 raid was not as successful as the 1929 foray, for in 1937 "prosperity" was an even more select and limited affair. Nevertheless the Kennecott company, which had made $25,500,000 in 1936, made $49,800,000 in 1937. And Anaconda's 1936 profit of $15,000,000 rose to $31,400,000 in 1937. Some of the profit increase came from larger volume, but most of it came from higher price.

Here again we have a situation in which prices do not fluctuate in accordance with costs. Any one of the large copper producers could have broken either the 1929 or the 1937 price-rises by the simple process of refusing to participate in them. Any producer could have sold for several cents under the peak prices and still have made a handsome profit on his sales. It is true that the top prices lasted for only a brief period. But they were broken by the resistance of the copper buyer, not by the independent action of any copper concern. Again the policy of the corporations is contradictory to the principles of competition, but is in perfect accord with the principles of monopoly. The industrialist shudders at the word "collectivism." Nevertheless he is operating with collectivized capital today.

Chapter V

THE "PRICE UMBRELLA" IN STEEL

In Discussing multiple monopoly in
the sulphur business and the copper business, I
have assumed that prices in these industries have
followed a course contrary to that which might
have been expected of them. But this assumption
of course depends upon the more basic assumption
that American industry is dominated by the competitive idea. From a more realistic standpoint
in which the monopolized character of large-scale
industry is taken into consideration, the price
trends in sulphur and copper are precisely what
could have been predicted. Nobody should be
surprised at price uniformity and price stability.
The astonishment should be reserved for those
occasions on which prices develop diversity and
fluctuation.

For just as the competitive system has its
philosophy and its theory, so also has the monopoly system. The monopoly theory has never
been much expounded because the people who

practice it cannot afford to admit that they are monopolistic. But although it has not been widely advertised, it is none the less powerful. It dominates every industry which can be entered only by means of a large investment of capital. It is based on the principle of safeguarding – and, if possible increasing – the investor's return on his investment. It does not much appeal to the highly individualistic industrialist like Mr. Ford because it subordinates the ego of the "enterpriser" to the welfare of the investor. But the capitalist realizes that all profit-making organisms live in glass houses and that none of them can afford to throw stones at the other. From his standpoint, a price battle between two large corporations would be suicide for both. He may have no theoretical objection to competition but experience has taught him that it is not profitable to compete. As far as the welfare of the investor is concerned, the capitalist's dislike of competition is thoroughly well founded. What happens to the welfare of society in general is something which will be discussed in a later section of this book. At the moment I should like to consider the development of an industry in which it is apparent that the abandonment of the competitive theory has not been a matter of chance or accident but a matter of careful planning and deliberate intent.

I refer to the steel industry which, under the leadership of the United States Steel Corp., has been the most significant example of planned monopoly that our industrial history affords.

In talking about the steel industry and U. S. Steel I should like to point out that neither the industry nor U. S. Steel is particularly a "big bad wolf" among our larger industrial animals. Whatever Big Steel may have been — or may have been intended to be — when the elder Morgan founded it, in recent years it has shown a surprising degree of enlightenment for an organization of its size and kind. Under the leadership of Board Chairman Myron Taylor it came to an agreement with the C.I.O. without causing any strikes or killing any strikers. To be sure, in so doing it only followed the laws of the United States, yet its conduct was so shocking to many members of the Iron and Steel Institute that the Morgan company was widely accused of having "betrayed" the industry. More recently, under the leadership of its present head, Edward Stettinius, Jr., U. S. Steel announced a marked reduction in prices without a corresponding reduction in wages. It may well be that the price cut was designed as a preliminary to a wage cut, but at least the corporation did cut the prices first. In the long run it does not make much difference whether a corporation is as benevolent as conditions permit or as vicious as circumstances allow. It is in the nature of a corporation to look out for its investors. Given a sufficient period of low earnings and no dividends, Mr. Stettinius would probably find himself forced into much the same position as that which Mr. Girdler, for example, needs little pressure to occupy. The fact that U. S. Steel has today an able and a relatively enlightened management merely accentuates the fact that the evil results of the monopoly system do not spring from bad men but from their bad system.

It is also a fortunate coincidence that the steel industry is often cited as an exception to monopolistic trends because the United States Steel Corp.'s share of the total business has been declining almost since its formation nearly forty years ago. When Big Steel was organized (1901) it owned two-thirds of the total steel capacity of the United States. It is still more than twice the size of its nearest competitor (Bethlehem), about four times the size of the next largest (Republic), seven to eight times the size of the rest of the larger "independents" (Jones and Laughlin, National, Youngstown, Inland, and American Rolling Mill). But its share of the total steel business has gone down until it now makes hardly more than

one-third (37%) of the national steel output.
Yet the steel industry has been a monopoly-industry ever since U. S. Steel was formed. And the
growth of the independent concerns is in itself
an example of, not an exception to, the way in
which an industrial monopoly operates. The independents did not prosper *in spite of* the U. S.
Steel Corp. They prospered *because of* the U. S.
Steel Corp. In Wall Street the steel industry is
commonly described as having grown up under
the "price umbrella" extended over it by U. S.
Steel. Some Wall Streeters think the umbrella
was too generous and that the big steel company
kept the little steel companies a touch too dry.
Others point out that the first duty of U. S. Steel
was to protect its own head. But neither group
disputes the existence of the "umbrella," or is
unaware of the fact that the modern steel industry is the product of the price policy initiated
by U. S. Steel. Let us take a look at the umbrella
and at the corporations grouped happily under it.

I am not going to re-tell the story of the formation of U. S. Steel; it has already been told many
times. It is, however, significant to recall that
the United States Steel Corp. was organized with
the purpose of eliminating price competition.
Even before the company went into production

the man who invested in it was assured that his capital was not being ventured in a freely competitive field. Otherwise he would not have put a penny into what would obviously have been a crazy scheme.

Prior to the formation of U. S. Steel, unrestricted competition had prevailed in the steel industry,* but to no good purpose from the steel producer's or investor's point of view. During the depression of the early Eighteen Nineties, a great many iron and steel companies had gone into bankruptcy and although Carnegie Steel had made a great deal of money the industry as a whole was in very bad shape. Furthermore, although smaller steel companies tended to disappear through failure or consolidation, the industry was solidifying not into one large unit but into two large units, Andrew Carnegie's Carnegie Steel and J. P. Morgan's Federal Steel. By the end of the century it was evident that these two companies would have to come to a showdown or come to an agreement. There was a possibility that Mr. Carnegie, the steel man, would ruin Mr. Morgan, the money man. There was a possibility that Mr. Morgan, the money man, would smash Mr. Carnegie, the steel man. Federal Steel already

---

* Though pools had been attempted, nobody had abided by the agreements.

represented a consolidation of many small companies into one big company. It was an early example of control by capital instead of control by management. But Mr. Carnegie was the rugged individualist of his period, the Henry Ford of steel.* And in the closing years of the nineteenth century that portion of the American public which took an interest in industrial affairs was speculating as to whether the two kinds of capitalism — monopolistic and competitive — would clash, and as to what the outcome might be.

As we now know, the showdown never came. Mr. Carnegie sold his company to Mr. Morgan and left monopoly capitalism in possession of the field. Not that Mr. Carnegie fared badly. He went back to Scotland with some $492,000,000 of the newly formed U. S. Steel Corp.'s stocks and bonds. And in selling out to the bankers Mr. Carnegie showed his usual good judgment. A fight between Carnegie Steel and Federal Steel would have resembled a head-on collision between two fast-moving locomotives. One might succeed in knocking the other off the track, but the winner would not come out in much better condition than the loser. But, however wise Mr. Carnegie's decision may have been, it marked the end of an era in

---

* The Carnegie company also contained many consolidated concerns, but remained dominated by Carnegie and tended toward monopoly by extinction rather than monopoly by cooperation.

American industrial life. It is true that in buying Carnegie Steel Mr. Morgan was following the classic line of monopoly development. He had eliminated Mr. Carnegie, although by purchase, not by force. Had the U. S. Steel Corp. then used its size and its resources to stamp out the smaller steel companies remaining in the industry, Mr. Morgan would merely have followed in Mr. Rockefeller's footsteps and no new economic development would have been made.

But Mr. Morgan — or Mr. Gary, the Morgan nominee who shortly became Chairman of the Board of U. S. Steel — followed precisely the opposite course. Not that he really had much choice in the matter. Mr. Rockefeller had already aroused public opinion against trusts. The Sherman Anti-Trust Act, forbidding "combinations in restraint of trade," had been passed in 1890 and Theodore Roosevelt was waving the Big Stick around so violently that there was always a possibility that he might misjudge his distance and actually hit somebody with it. From the time of its formation, U. S. Steel was worried about being prosecuted under the Sherman act, and from its beginning it took very good care to furnish no evidence that it was monopolizing the steel industry. When the Government finally did bring suit against U. S. Steel (in 1911) the Supreme Court acquitted the corporation on the ground that size in itself was not a violation of the law and that the Government had not shown that U. S. Steel was using any unfair methods to crush its competitors. So one reason why Big Steel did not become an old-time monopoly was that it knew better than to try.

There was also the problem of whether U. S. Steel could *afford* to undersell its scattered but numerous competitors. It had bought up a great many small companies in order to become the No. 1 company and many of these companies were more impressive on paper than in operation. Many of them were high-cost producers with antiquated equipment. U. S. Steel also started out in life with the handicap of a tremendous overcapitalization. The money invested in its stocks and bonds was about twice as great as the value of its plant and other tangible assets. But it had to pay the interest on its $400,000,000 in bonds and it was under a practical compulsion to pay some dividends on its billion dollars' worth of stock, particularly on the preferred stock.* So, to keep its investors happy,

* A bondholder is a creditor of a corporation, entitled to his interest, come hell or high water. A shareholder is technically a partner; the corporation does not owe him any dividends (in the sense of a legal debt) no matter how small his return on his investment may be. But a corporation cannot afford to pass dividends habitually. For then its old investors will not invest more of their money in it and neither can it attract new investors. It will find itself unable to secure more capital — and capital is what all corporations always want.

it had to show not only large sales but also large profits. Its size was considered a guarantee of satisfactory sales volume. But its size would also tend to reduce the profit of the sales. It was a sprawly, cumbersome outfit; it had too many plants, they were too scattered to operate in a completely unified way; some of the equipment should have been in a museum, and the controlling brains of the company were in Wall Street, not in Pittsburgh. Big Steel was therefore in no mood to price-cut the independent steel companies into submission or extinction. In fact, what the corporation desired was not price *cutting* but price *fixing*. The compensating factor for high costs and overcapitalization is found in high, steady prices. So from its beginnings U. S. Steel has advocated a firm price structure for the entire industry.

Big Steel did not object if other companies made money under this arrangement. It was not run by any industrial ego-maniac, consumed by an ambition to make all the steel in the country. It knew that its policies were encouraging its competitors. It realized that closely knit, well managed, owner-operated steel companies could turn out steel at lower costs. Obviously these companies would make more profit per dollar sale than U. S. Steel could make. They would grow more rapidly than U. S. Steel. They might eventually cut into U. S. Steel's share of the steel market. But what of it? The market (in 1901) was rapidly increasing; until as recently as 1929 it was assumed that the market would always increase. U. S. Steel was, and still is, incomparably the No. 1 steel producer. So the growth of the independent did not matter; even the dog in the manger prob ably would not have been so inhospitable if the manger was getting bigger all the time. In any event, U. S. Steel knew it would be wise to co-operate with the rest of the industry.

Why, then, did not the independents, perceiving the disadvantages of the No. 1 company, sell as close to cost as possible and free the industry from its "trust menace" by putting U. S. Steel out of business entirely? If U. S. Steel was not strong enough to fight the independents, why were not the independents strong enough to fight U. S. Steel? According to the orthodox economic theory they should have closed in on Big Steel and under-sold it off the map. But this theory is merely the other side of the theory we have just been discussing. It, too, is based on the competitive concept. It, too, depends upon the underlying assumption that somebody is trying to put somebody else out of business. This time the little fellow is picked as the winner. But the truth is that there can be neither winner nor loser, for the reason that there is no fight.

In the first place, it must be remembered that

there is no such thing as a small steel company, in the sense that there is a small drugstore or a small cigar stand. National Steel, for instance, has only about one-seventh the capacity of U. S. Steel, but more than $50,000,000 are invested in it. Any company large enough to produce enough steel to be visible to the naked eye has the same problem as U. S. Steel itself in the way of protecting its investment and paying its dividends.

In the second place, a man cannot sell what he cannot make, and steel capacity cannot be enlarged overnight. The steel industry today has a capacity of around 70 million tons of steel, of which Big Steel can produce some 26 million. Suppose you had a steel mill with a capacity of a million tons. And suppose that steel (billets) were selling (as they commonly do sell) for $37 a ton. You might very possibly be able to quote a $35-a-ton price and still make a healthy profit. But you could not sell more than a million tons of steel no matter how low your prices, for although you might get orders for more steel you could not fill them. Even if you re-invested all your profits in the business (depriving your stockholders of their dividends) it would take you a good many years to step up your capacity to a point where you could make appreciable inroads on the sales of the larger concerns. And long before that point was reached, they would have cracked you on the head by bringing their prices down to yours until you became sensible enough to put your prices back up with theirs.

This is really the more significant point. The price advantage of the smaller but more efficient company can exist only so long as the bigger and less efficient companies permit it. It would not be tolerated for a very long period, yet it could exist only on a toleration basis. We have said that U. S. Steel was a high-cost producer, and there is no doubt but that if the independents had combined against it and forced a price war, Mr. Morgan's big company would have lost a lot of money. As a matter of fact, there was little likelihood of any such combination, for the independents themselves had just come out of a long period of competition and depression in which they had come to regard price cutting as a practice much akin to throat cutting. But *had* the independents, or any considerable group of them, fought Big Steel, obviously the No. 1 company would have been forced to fight back. It did not want a fight. A fight would have cost it hundreds of millions of dollars. But though it did not want to lose money it had, in a pinch, the money to lose. After all, a billion and a half dollars had been put into the company and the investors would, if necessary, have put in another billion and a half to preserve their original investment. It is only in the fairy stories that Jack climbs the beanstalk to pick on the giant, and although it is possible that in this case there were enough Jacks finally to get the giant down, the giant would account for a great many of his attackers before his finish came. Backed into a corner, U. S. Steel would have met anybody's prices, at no matter what loss, and it always had an excellent chance of emerging as the lone survivor of the bloody field.

The better strategy from the standpoint of both the little steel companies and the big steel company was to play "you post your price and I'll post your price." The steel market was growing rapidly during the first twenty-nine years of the present century. Everybody was reasonably certain to get his share of the business; why should anybody chisel on his prices to get a little more? Besides, in the long run, the independent could cut in on Big Steel's percentage of the total business in a way that company would not resent. For the low-cost company would, as we have already observed, make more profit per dollar sale than U. S. Steel. (In 1937, for instance, U. S. Steel made about $8\frac{1}{2}$ cents net per dollar sale; Ernest Weir's National Steel, probably the lowest-cost large-scale producer in the field, made about

12 cents per dollar sale.) Its return on its investment would be very good and, in addition to the part of its profits which it might use for plant expansion, it would also be able to sell new stock and new bonds to new investors and thus get more capital for new factories and new furnaces. Meanwhile U. S. Steel would be making satisfactory profits, it would always have a great appeal to the more conservative investor, and though the smaller companies might be growing more rapidly, there would be no reason for the big company to become excited and attempt reprisals.

Steel prices were therefore fixed at a figure sufficient to give nearly every steel producer a profit. Those with lower production costs realized on their advantage by making greater profits per dollar of sale, not by attempting a rapid expansion of sales through lower prices per ton of steel. In the fifteen-year period before 1900, when the steel business was competitive, the price of steel rails varied from $34.52 a ton to $17.62 a ton. Between 1902 and 1916, when the steel business was monopolistic, they stayed at $28 a ton. We have already referred to the average price of steel during the depression and noted that even when the industry was operating at hardly more than one-eighth of its capacity it was still selling steel at over three-fourths of 1929 prices.

Remember that uniform prices are not a matter of coercion but a matter of cooperation. Big Steel may have coaxed the industry into stabilizing its prices, but no bullying was involved. You do not have to threaten a man to make him do something which he can see is profitable for him. Nor do you have to sign any documents or swear any oaths to make him follow a policy which is to his advantage as well as to yours. Old John D. Rockefeller was the classic monopolist, but Mr. Rockefeller moved toward monopoly by making competition so stiff that his competitors could not stand it. But Mr. Rockefeller was an individualist. He was working for his company, for himself. The modern investor does not care where his money goes as long as it discovers a safe refuge in which to breed dividends. He does not care how much profit other dollars make, so long as his dollars make profits too. He approves of a competitor as long as the competitor disapproves of competition,

I should like to cite one more example of monopoly tactics and monopoly prices because it affords a striking instance of monopoly profits. If you were asked whether the cigarette industry or the automobile industry made the more money, you would almost certainly pick the automobile industry. And, most of the time, you would be correct. The auto industry represents incomparably the greater investment, employment, and sales. It ordinarily returns many times the profit. But let us look at some auto profits and cigarette profits over a period of years. The following table shows the profits (as compiled by Standard Statistics Co.) of a group of seven cigarette manufacturers and 12 automobile companies:

Year	Cigarette Profits	Auto Profits
1926	$70,000,000	$250,000,000
1927	75,000.000	290,000,000
1928	80,000,000	365,000,000
1929	85,000,000	330,000,000
1930	105,000,000	165,000,000
1931	110,000,000	90,000,000
1932	105,000,000	def. 30,000,000
1933	60,000,000	90,000,000
1934	70,000,000	95,000,000
1935	69,000,000	200,000,000

We see that in 1931 and 1932 the cigarette business made more money than the auto business and that in 1933 and in 1934 the cigarette did very well in comparison to the motor car. On the other hand, cigarette profits were far below auto profits in the good years, and in the recovery period the motor car again left the cigarette far behind.

The explanation lies in the fact that the cigarette companies did not have any depression. From 1927 through 1929 they made $240,000,000. From 1930 through 1932 they made $320,000,000. In the three "bad" years they made $80,000,000 more than they had made in the three "good" years. They made 33% more money in three depression years than in three prosperity years. How were they able to defy the law of financial gravity? For the reason that cigarettes are sold in a monopoly market, but tobacco is bought in a competitive market. Throughout the depression, Camels, Luckies, Chesterfields, and Old Golds — the Big Four of the industry — sold at their "standard" price of around 15 cents a pack. But there was no "standard" price for tobacco. The price of tobacco went from about 18 cents a pound in 1929 to about 10.5 cents a pound in 1932. Cigarettes are almost entirely machine made. Labor costs do not amount to more than 5% of total costs. The cost of the raw material is the dominating factor in cigarette profits. Thus the American Tobacco Co. (Luckies), R. J. Reynolds Tobacco Co. (Camels), Liggett & Myers Tobacco Co. (Chesterfields), and P. Lorillard Co. (Old Golds), were coining money by putting 10-cents-a-pound tobacco into 15-cents-a-pack cigarettes. Their profits show that all of them, or any of them, could have reduced their prices greatly, with plenty of profit margin left. But they preferred—and all of them preferred—to charge prosperity prices and to make more than prosperity profits.

The social aspects of this policy are not improved by the fact that all the companies are fragments of the old tobacco trust (James B. Duke's original American Tobacco Co.) which was solemnly dissolved by the courts in 1912. Yet although the old trust was divided into several pieces, we have just seen how little you can foster competition by division. Furthermore, the stockholders in the old trust lost no part of their ownership by its dissolution. They got shares in the "pieces" in proportion to their holdings in the original company. Thus all the big cigarette companies are paying a considerable portion of their dividends to the Duke family (big stockholders in the original monopoly) and hence Doris Duke's position as "richest girl in the world." But I suppose that cigarettes are not exactly a necessity of life and at the moment I am more interested in the technique than in the ethics of monopoly production.

The big 1933 decline in cigarette profits is also significant. In 1933 the "leading" companies made $60,000,000 as compared to $105,000,000 the year before. Here also they went against the prevailing trend, for the rest of the country was just beginning to stagger out of its depression low. The profits of the cigarette companies dropped in 1933 because the price of tobacco was brought back to something approaching a "normal" figure. In 1933, tobacco got back to 13 cents a pound; by 1935 it was up to 21.3 cents, and the cigarette profit slumped accordingly. Notice how the profits of these companies went in the opposite direction from the income of the tobacco farmer. When the tobacco grower was in a desperate condition, unable to get enough money for his crop to pay his operating costs and interest charges, the cigarette companies flourished like the green bay tree. When the Government gave the tobacco grower a helping hand, the swollen profits of the cigarette companies went down to their usual size. Here is a good example of the clash of interest between the monopoly and the public. The cigarette companies did not care what happened to the farmer as long as their profits went up. They took advantage of his depression to put on a private boom all their own. But, it will be argued, what else could you expect them to do? Business is business, is it not? That, unfortunately, is just the trouble. Business has a habit of insisting upon being business until it becomes a bad business for you and me. And often a bad business for itself as well.

I have said so much about monopoly industry that it is perhaps desirable to remind the reader that competitive industry still exists. Remember that most of the corporations in this country are still doing business in the competitive way. Remember our dual system of monopoly operating side by side with competition. But also keep in mind the fact that it is the monopoly companies that are monopolizing the profits. Some of them are "natural" monopolies, like American Telephone, the big light and power companies, and such railroads as have not abused their position by reckless overconstruction and fantastic overcapitalization. Some of them are patent monopolies, like the Aluminum Co. and the Radio Corporation and Gillette Razor and Eastman Kodak. Most of them belong in the "multiple monopoly" class — in industries dominated by a few large producers and characterized by high, uniform prices that rarely slip.

The only strictly competitive enterprises which consistently turn in multi-million-dollar profits are those which operate on such a tremendous scale that even a very small profit per dollar results in a large number of total dollars made. In 1937, the Great Atlantic and Pacific Tea Co., for instance, made about $9,000,000 on about $880,-000,000 of sales, netting about 1 cent profit per dollar sale. The A. and P. may be a menace to the small retailer, yet it does operate competitively in a competitive field. Meanwhile, in the same year, General Electric, on sales of $350,000,-000, made $63,000,000 net. General Electric does 15% of the total business in its field and has only one competitor (Westinghouse) of comparable size. It made 18 cents per dollar sale and it sold most of its products under price-structure protection.

The competitive system has not disappeared and it can indefinitely survive. But the vitality has gone out of it. It never held much attraction for big capital and it holds even less today. For, as the capitalist has revised the Bible, "Competition killeth but monopoly giveth life."

Chapter VI

THE DECLINE OF THE CORPORATE MANAGER

THERE was a time when the men who managed American corporations were also the men who founded and owned them. This condition still exists in small and medium-sized businesses. That it exists with respect to all companies is a fiction often advanced by persons who believe – or pretend to believe – in the individualism of American industry. But our older and larger companies have outlived their founders and outgrown their managers. In 1931, Gerard Lambert was made president of the Gillette Safety Razor Co. Mr. Lambert had never previously been associated either with the late King Gillette or with the razor blade company. He did not get his job because he owned any Gillette stock. Mr. Lambert had made his reputation selling Listerine – a mouth-wash purchased by millions of persons who had read about halitosis in Listerine advertisements. The Gillette company needed a high pressure salesman, so Mr. Lambert was called in. No doubt Mr. Lambert was a very good razor-salesman. But it would be hard to consider him as the entrepreneur of the razor company. He was, as he would be the first to admit, not the boss of the concern. He was working for the stockholders. Or, more accurately, for a few large stockholders who owned enough shares in the company to make their influence felt. And such is commonly the position of the men who manage the really big business of today.

Another of our fine old corporate leaders (although for the past eleven years it has been most conspicuous for its deficits) is the American Woolen Co. The entrepreneur of this concern — a merger of many New England woolen mills — was the late William Madison Wood, who shot himself in 1926. Mr. Wood had many of the characteristics of the traditional captain of industry, although perhaps not the characteristics which have been most publicized in most captains. Thus, in addition to what was reported to be a million dollar per annum salary, Mr. Wood was also said to have had his life insurance premiums paid by the company. Like nearly all the other corporate managers of his time, he was an ardent expansionist and, for a while, his expansions prospered. But the woolen industry was among the first of our industries to feel the consequences of over-building during the war-time boom. The amount of clothing worn by women decreased. Rayon appeared as a competitive textile. There was a remarkable growth of a low-cost textile industry in the South. American Woolen had therefore its private depression before industry in general declined. All of which was unfortunate for Mr. Wood's lasting reputation among the industrial great.

Mr. Wood is not, however, the subject of my American Woolen story. My point is that our large companies are now, for the most part, managed by men who have arrived since the captains and the kings departed. There has been a succession of American Woolen Co. presidents since Mr. Wood's departure. Among them was Lionel Noah, who arrived at 1931. The American Woolen Co. had by that time accumulated a string of very large deficits; the entire woolen industry was in a bad way; and Mr. Noah was taking over a tough job. To make the job less unattractive, the woolen company offered Mr. Noah a bonus deal; that is, it offered to split with him a portion of whatever profits it might make. Such deals were common during the prosperity period — Eugene Grace of Bethlehem collected more than $1,500,000 on one in 1929 and for some years a "management bonus" plan has enriched the leading executives of General Motors.

In fairness to Mr. Noah, it should be said that the American Woolen plan was in no sense a method of letting him in on a guaranteed good thing. It was so long since American Woolen had made any money that many people thought it never would show a profit again. And 1931 was no year in which any money-losing company might be expected to mend its ways. Nor – in 1931 or in 1932 – did American Woolen. But in 1933 the company turned in a profit of $7,000,000 and Mr. Noah's long shot came handsomely in. For in the summer of 1933 the New Deal came along with its National Industrial Recovery Act, a measure designed to raise and to maintain prices. The price of wool shot up 87 per cent and the American Woolen Co., which had a large inventory of raw wool bought at pre-NRA prices, made it up into finished wool at post-NRA prices and prospered mightily. To be sure, the profit was what balance sheets call non-recurring, i.e., something that only happens once. The next year the American Woolen Co. quickly reverted to its losing ways and in 1936 Mr. Noah left.

Here again, perhaps, the narrative has obscured the moral of my story. As an American Woolen stockholder, I should much prefer President Noah to President Wood. (In 1933 I might have preferred President Roosevelt.) Nevertheless, Mr. Wood was the organizer, the enterpriser, the rugged individualist of the concern. Mr. Noah (like Mr. Lambert of Gillette) was strictly a newcomer. He had been imported from Gimbel's (Philadelphia) Department Store on the perfectly correct theory that American Woolen needed somebody who knew what the public wanted, not somebody who knew how to manufacture woolen cloth. Whoever controlled American Woolen stock gave him the job, just as they afterwards gave it to somebody else. In the typical American corporation of today the divorce between ownership and management has become almost complete.

But when we say that the stockholders of a company are the owners of the company, of course we do not mean that "the public" is the owner. I suppose that the nearest approach we have made to public ownership in this country is the mutual life insurance company, like the Equitable or the Metropolitan. Here every policyholder is a stockholder and even the man with the largest policy is lost among the hundreds of thousands of his fellow-owners. But it is impossible for such a large and scattered group to think together or act together. So, oddly enough, the only type of big business which may truly be called "publicly held" in the sense that ownership is *evenly* divided among hundreds of thousands of small stockholders, is also the only type of large business which the management may truly be said to run. As a policy holder of the Metropolitan, I might violently have disapproved of Mr. Leroy Lincoln as its new president, or of his $120,000 a year salary. But trying to elect a candidate against Mr. Lincoln would be a job about on a par with trying to elect a governor of a state. It would cost me hundreds of thousands of dollars to reach, let alone convince, my fellow proprietors that somebody else would do a better job. So I let some small group of influential persons, presumably the gentlemen on the Board of Directors, name Mr. Lincoln or whomever they choose to name, and go my way, a very absentee landlord indeed.

In the more usual forms of big business, however, the stock is very far from equally divided among the stockholders. Here a small minority of the proprietors have acquired the proprietary rights. In a previous chapter (*The Distribution of Dividends*) we have shown what a large percentage of the ownership of big business lies in the hands of a few rich men. These men, naturally enough, take a lively interest in the affairs of the corporations whose stock they own in such large blocks. They are truly the investors. They personify capital.

And they are the real bosses of every company which they and others like them control. They do not care what the company makes, provided it makes money. (Whereas Henry Ford, for instance, one of the few survivors of the founder-manager type, presumably would not be happy making money out of Eskimo Pies.) They do not care who is the president of the company, provided he supplies them with dividends. They hire presidents with the same ease that an office manager hires office boys. And the president does not hold office for any longer than he can keep his pencil sharp.

The capitalist is rarely found among the operating officers of his company. But he is always well represented on its Board of Directors. Thus some Morgan man (for a brief period it was J. P. Morgan himself) has been Chairman of the Board of U. S. Steel since its formation in 1901. After Judge Gary, Morgan spokesman, died in 1927, the Steel Corporation policies were determined by Morgan designate Myron Taylor. Eventually Mr. Taylor retired, but another Morgan man, Edward Stettinius, Jr. succeeded him. Meanwhile there have been many presidents of U. S. Steel, but it has never made very much difference just who the president might be. When U. S. Steel decided to come to terms with the C.I.O., it was Myron Taylor who carried on the negotiations with John

L. Lewis. Presumably, the first thing that Benjamin Fairless, current president of U. S. Steel, heard about the Taylor-Lewis conversations was that an agreement had been reached and that he should forthwith recognize the C. I. O.

Not that the corporation president has nothing to do, once he gets the job, or that he commonly leads a dull life. Before the depression, to be sure, he usually inherited an established concern, a practically guaranteed share of the business in his industry, a "firm" price structure, and what appeared to be certain profits.

There was a man named Seger who was the head of the United States Rubber Co. during most of the 1920's. U. S. Rubber was known as the Rubber Trust back in the days when boots and shoes were the chief rubber products. It was a ponderous and slow-moving object with more water in its stock than you could have poured into its boots. When the auto tire appeared as the main customer for rubber, U. S. Rubber lost its dominating position in the rubber industry, for tire-specialists like Goodyear, Goodrich, and Firestone came up to share the top rank. But U. S. Rubber, of course, also produced tires (U. S. Royals were and are its No. 1 brand) and, for several years, made a great deal more money with shoes and tires than it had ever made on shoes alone. It had a preferred stock on which it had never passed a dividend since 1904, it was still the biggest rubber company, and it went its way in apparent security and unquestionable dignity.

It had, as became it, its own building (1790 Broadway) on the top floor of which was Mr. Seger's office. While Mr. Seger was going to and from it, one of the elevators in the building was reserved for Mr. Seger's private use. None of the thousands of other persons who worked in the U. S. Rubber building could then occupy it. It took Mr. Seger up in the morning and down alone at noon. It took him up after lunch and down in the evening alone. It was not an elevator. It was a symbol. It represented the dignity of office.

The elevator is still running, but it is just an elevator now. There is still a U. S. Rubber building, but the company has rented much of the space. For even before the depression had become general, U. S. Rubber was feeling depressed. It was plagued with repeated losses on inventory. It had a bonded debt that made it look more like a railroad than a manufacturing company. And it was in one of the few large industries in which the competitors insisted on competing.* It had to pay its bond interest and it was too proud not to pay the dividend

---

* Mr. Harvey Firestone has often been "blamed" for the fact that tire companies actually did indulge in price wars and other pre-Twentieth Century forms of competition. Within the past few years, however, the tire industry appears to have seen the light and Wall Streeters no longer regard Mr. Firestone as a lone wolf of Akron.

on its famous ever-paying preferred. By the time that business in general was bad, business at U. S. Rubber was terrible, and in January, 1929 Mr. Seger rode down alone on his elevator for the last time. The E. I. du Pont de Nemours family (*not* the du Pont company) bought into U. S. Rubber and put Mr. Francis B. Davis, Jr., for many years a Du Pont company executive, in Mr. Seger's place. And all Mr. Davis asks of an elevator at any time is that it should be able to go up and down.

Of course, as we have seen in previous chapters, there are a number of companies which supplied their presidents with good things that remained good things: it would be quite difficult to lose money with Eastman Kodak, United Shoe Machinery, Coca-Cola, or any number of big earners, in good times or bad. And there were presidents who, having produced many large dividends during the boom period, survived the depression even though their dividends shrank.

There is currently, moreover, a large group of what might be called Depression Presidents who came into office when things were at their worst and thus had the great advantage of being almost certain to improve upon their predecessors. A great deal of nonsense has been talked and printed about the "management factor" — i.e., the ability of President A to make money where President B or

President C would have lost it. In nearly every case, President A will do exactly what any other member of the alphabet would have done in his position, for the earnings of any large corporation are determined chiefly by industry conditions and not by the individual ability of the company's operating head. Daniel Willard has been head of the Baltimore & Ohio for 28 years, but the B & O has had many ups and downs since Willard took charge. Lately it has been leaning heavily on money borrowed from the government, but as recently as 1929 it made $28,700,000. Eugene Grace was head of Bethlehem Steel in 1929 when it made $42,200,000. He was also its president in 1932, when it lost $19,400,000. He still had the job in 1937, when Bethlehem's earnings were $31,800,-000. The earnings of one large company rise and fall with the earnings of all large companies in the industry allowing for the fact that certain companies are inherently good earners and other companies are inherently bad earners. Nobody could fail to show a large profit running the R. J. Reynolds Tobacco Co. (Camel cigarettes) but anybody who could coax dividends out of the Pittsburgh Coal Co., the International Mercantile Marine Co., or similar industrial cripples would be a remarkable corporate manager indeed.

Remember, I am not discussing the men who

founded companies on the strength of some original concept. Edison and Westinghouse were great inventors, although neither was a good corporate manager and both lost control of the companies which bore their names.* Frank Woolworth had an idea that a store in which everything sold for five cents (the dime was an afterthought) might be successful. John D. Rockefeller, Sr.'s, big idea — that it would be excellent for him to refine all the petroleum produced in America — was less individual, but no one can deny that the old Standard Oil Co. was little more than Mr. Rockefeller in an incorporated form. And so on. Some of the old-time "empire builders" employed methods which nowadays would land them in jail; some of them depended upon natural resources and the growth of the population; none of them thought of sharing any of his power until he became decrepit. They are more romantic in retrospect than they

---

* There is here a problem in nomenclature. Mr. Edison founded several Edison companies. The first and most important is now known as the General Electric Co. It used to be the *Edison* General Electric Co. but in 1892, to Mr. Edison's horror, the company merged with the Thomson-Houston Co. and the Edison name dropped out of the title of the merged concern. The Edison electric-light patents, however, were retained. To the present Thomas A. Edison, Inc., I have no reference.

There are also two Westinghouse companies, Westinghouse Air Brake and Westinghouse Electric & Manufacturing. Mr. Westinghouse was head of the Air Brake company at the time of his death in 1914. Control of the Electric & Manufacturing company, however, passed out of his hands in the 1907 reorganization.

were in reality. But each could at least have said of his company, "A poor thing, but mine own."

Today the president of the large corporation is — with a few conspicuous but aged exceptions — a hired man. There is a story about an executive who was head of a steel company during the worst years of the depression. He was running up some good sized deficits, through no particular fault of his, and the stockholders were yelling for his head. Not the little stockholders (they were angry, too, but not important) but the big stockholders, the men who were on, or who were represented on, the board of directors. The steel president came out of a meeting of the directors one day in a very stormy mood. After all, he did not start the depression and all the other steel companies were having their headaches too.

"My God," he said, "what do they expect of me? Miracles? I'm doing all anybody could do for $45,000 a year."

There are few better examples of the transition from owner-management to banker-management than the history of the Johns-Manville Corp. This corporation specializes in all manner of things that have an insulation value. One of its major assets is its asbestos mine in Quebec. The outstanding characteristic of asbestos is its resistance to heat. Boilers and pipes are insulated with asbestos. Asbestos shingles provide a fire-proof roof. Asbestos enables brake linings to stand up under the high temperatures generated by the friction which stops your car. Not everything that Johns-Manville makes has asbestos in it, but asbestos remains the basic material in the Johns-Manville world.

The Johns-Manville Corp. dates from 1901, when the H. W. Johns Manufacturing Co. (roofing) and the Manville Covering Co.(insulation) merged. From 1901 to 1925 the dominating figure in the company was Thomas F. Manville, who ran it strictly as a one-man show. Like most of the industrialists of his period, he was a pronounced egotist whose pride in his company reflected his pride in himself. When, for instance, he went to visit his plant at Manville, New Jersey, he found that accommodations for over-night visitors were very limited. So he built, at Manville, a fine, spacious hotel. Now this town, as the name indicates, is merely an adjunct of the Manville plant. Very few visitors come there except on Johns-Manville business. Mr. Manville's hotel, as a hotel, was a money-loser from its beginning. But this did not bother Mr. Manville. When he and his friends and his customers went down to Manville, they did not have to stay at any tank-town inn. A metropolitan hotel awaited them. When they went back to New York, the hotel was again empty. But its emptiness was not a matter of importance. The situation required a gesture, and an appropriate, if expensive, gesture had been made. Meanwhile the company was steadily increasing its output, its sales, and its profit. Mr. Manville was perhaps a little extravagant about the hotel, but it was an extravagance which the business could well afford. In the mid nineteen-twenties, the Johns-Manville company was an example of American industrial individualism, a company which from a very small beginning had grown into a large corporation under twenty-five years of one-man management.

Growing up along with — but far away from — the Johns-Manville company was Lewis Herold Brown, who was working in a corrugated-paper factory in Iowa at the time when the United States declared war on Germany. Mr. Brown joined the A. E. F., became a Captain at the age of 23, survived the perils of war, and after the Armistice started back to Iowa. In Chicago, between trains, Mr. Brown took a sight-seeing trip through the plant of Montgomery Ward, the second largest mail order house in the country (Sears, Roebuck being the largest). Mr. Brown liked what he saw, decided that he could get along without Iowa, and talked the mail order people into giving him a job.

In 1921 Montgomery Ward, like many another company in that panic year, got into trouble and came out of it with a new president. The new president, Theodore F. Merseles, was a selection of the House of Morgan. I do not know when J. P. Morgan & Co. acquired an interest in Montgomery Ward, but at any rate they were evidently in a position to name its president, for Mr. Merseles was unquestionably a Morgan man. He had made an excellent reputation as head of the old National Cloak and Suit Co., a New York mail order house specializing in apparel. He did not like Chicago. (In fact, his family stayed in New York and Mr. Merseles commuted back and forth every other week end.) But the panic of 1921 was short-lived; by 1922 prosperity was on its way back again; and Mr. Merseles, much as he disliked his environment, did very well with his job. Mr. Brown also prospered, working his way up to the position of Assistant to the President.

In 1925, Mr. Manville was seized with a heart attack and died. His brother, Hiram E. Manville, became head of the company; but he was already an elderly man and had no desire to hold the position on more than a pro-tem basis. Logical successor, by inheritance, was Thomas Manville, Jr., but Tommy Manville had already broken into the public prints in rather conspicuous ways and did not seem to be the ideal candidate for the office. Finally Hiram Manville, who himself had considerable holdings in the company, rounded up enough additional stock from a group of older executives and from Tommy himself to get control of the concern. And, in 1927, he sold his holdings to J. P. Morgan & Co., who acquired 400,000 of the 750,000 shares then outstanding.

Forthwith, the Morgan partners recalled Mr. Merseles from Chicago and made him president of the Johns-Manville concern. This step violently displeased the best minds around the Johns-Manville office, since they had assumed that any shift of management would result in a new president chosen from the men who had grown up with asbestos. They accused Hiram Manville of having sold them down the river and for a long time Mr. Merseles was a very unpopular chief executive. Nevertheless, Mr. Merseles came and remained. And the one man whom he brought along with him from Chicago was Lewis Herold Brown. Assistant to Mr. Merseles in Chicago, Mr. Brown continued as assistant to Mr. Merseles in New York.

For the next two years, Johns-Manville went through a period of careful pruning. Mr. Merseles was essentially an efficiency expert, a shrewd manager. Old Thomas Manville had thought of more and more things for the Johns-Manville company to make. At one point there were 2200 items in the company's catalogue. They included a line of fire extinguishers. Most of the Johns-Manville products were, as we have seen, sold on a heat-preservation or fire-protection basis. The asbestos shingles in particular sold on their fire-proof nature. But asbestos shingles were a very expensive form of roof-covering and even the Johns-Manville salesmen could not supply all buildings with an asbestos roof. So, to sell something to those unregenerates who would not properly fire-proof themselves, Mr. Manville compromised with fire extinguishers. Mr. Merseles gave up the fire extinguishers, cut the catalogue items from 2200 to 1400. .

The story now takes one of those twists which the fiction writer would scorn to employ. You will remember that Mr. Manville died of heart failure in 1925. In the spring of 1929 Mr. Merseles, visiting some new Johns-Manville acquisitions in California, also had a heart attack and died at the Del Monte hotel. The Johns-Manville presidency had again become open and through another Act of God.

But this time there was only one possible successor — Mr. Brown. He was the only other Morgan man in the place; the remaining executives still resented the 1927 deal. So Mr. Brown, from

Iowa and Chicago, became Johns-Manville head. It is a position which he still occupies today.

I should say that Mr. Brown was an extremely competent corporation manager. He inherited his job only a few months before the big break in the stock market, and with the arrival of the depression plans for Johns-Manville expansion were laid aside. Most of Mr. Brown's administration has been spent in the disagreeable task of avoiding deficits. In 1937 the company turned in a profit of $4,500,000, but in 1938 bad times were back again and Mr. Brown had another hard row to hoe. In 1937, however, he had a $112,600 salary on which to hoe it.

The story of the Johns-Manville Corp. well illustrates the progress of a typical American concern. There is an old proverb about American families going from shirt-sleeves to shirt-sleeves in three generations, the point being that Father makes the money, Son spends it, and Grandson starts out again from scratch. There may have been merit in this saying at some previous date in our history, and it may still apply to the relatively modest fortunes which may be accumulated in the owner-managed concern. But the classic development of our larger corporations has been, not from small to big to small again, but from small to big to bigger yet. The step from big to bigger is almost always achieved by the introduction of outside credit. The business outgrows the money of its original owners. Then its need for money exceeds the lending ability of the local banks. Finally the head of the corporation decides to do some public financing. At this point, unless he is wealthy enough to take up a large portion of the new stock himself, or tricky enough to sell to outsiders a non-voting stock, the control of the company remains no longer with him. The point at which the industrialist sells out to the capitalist has been reached and passed by nearly every American corporation of the first rank.

How much difference it makes to you and to me whether the Johns-Manville company is controlled by Mr. Manville or by Mr. Morgan is, perhaps, a matter of opinion. The owner-managed corporation is not necessarily any more enlightened than the banker-managed corporation. Mr. Ford is certainly his own boss, and his stockholders (Mrs. Ford and Edsel Ford) are hardly in a position to put much dividend pressure on him. Yet Mr. Ford is among the conspicuously backward employers with respect to his attitude toward unions, whereas the Morgan partners (as evidenced by the U. S. Steel Corp.'s willingness to deal with the C.I.O.) exhibit a relatively enlightened point of view. If we could eliminate our present problems of monopoly capitalism we should merely find ourselves confronted with the problems of competitive capitalism. We should certainly not discover ourselves in any promised land.

But because the public, perhaps mistakenly, is better disposed toward the industrialist than toward the capitalist, the latter always hides behind the former when the two find themselves in the public eye. And it is important to realize that all this talk about individual initiative and rugged individualism and unregimented Americanism and all the rest of it is, under contemporary conditions, nonsense. When we think of big business today we should not think of it in terms of the big business man, no matter how many secretaries he may keep busy or how many telephones he may have on his desk. The large corporation of today is not the product of individual effort. It is the product of pooled capital. It is an example of concentrated and collectivized wealth.

Chapter VII

OVERPRODUCTION AND UNDERCONSUMPTION—THE AUTO INDUSTRY

THERE is a good deal to be said for the theory that the prosperity of the 1920's travelled on four wheels and was propelled by gasoline. If you believe with me that the prosperity itself was fundamentally unsound, I do not mind being considered a subscriber to the theory for, although it is something of an over-simplification, it explains a great deal. And the automobile industry sheds an even more brilliant light upon what happened in 1937 and 1938 than upon what happened in 1929 and 1930. The picture of industry during the 1920's roaring along in a high powered motor car, going faster and faster until the inevitable crash, is as nearly true as any such analogy can be. But the picture of industry in the last quarter of 1936 and the first quarter of 1937, hauled out of its ditch by the New Deal and careening off on the same old joyride, is even more significant. It demonstrates the inadvisability of giving a drunken driver another car.

The auto industry, as the epitome of industries, might reasonably be expected to produce the epitome of corporations. And the expectation has been fully realized. I suppose that if, before the World War, anyone had predicted that a single American corporation would ever make as much as $200,000,000 a year, that man would have been considered an industrial Jules Verne. Yet General Motors made $235,000,000 in 1927; $276,000,000 in 1928; and $248,000,000 in 1929. For the three years, its profits came to over three-quarters of a billion dollars. And even this remarkable record was — considering the changed character of the times — surpassed in more recent years. For the big auto company made, as I have pointed out elsewhere, $238,000,000 in 1936 and $196,000,000 in 1937. And except for a very bad fourth quarter in 1937, it would undoubtedly have broken the $200,000,000 mark in both years.

There has never been a profit maker like General Motors; even American Telephone, a national monopoly with a semi-guaranteed income, surpasses it only in years of most acute depression and no other manufacturing company is in General Motors' class. It has given the world a new concept of profits and dividends. It has also provided invaluable evidence concerning the problems of overproduction, unemployment, forced selling, and the maldistribution of wealth. Furthermore, in relegating Henry Ford to the position of a very bad second in the auto field, it has shown that even the most vigorous exponent of old-style individual industrialism cannot hold his own with the new style collective capitalism.* No matter what point one may wish to make about industry over the past fifteen years, General Motors is almost certain to be the best example of it.

Let us first consider some of the reasons why the automobile has been so commonly considered the chariot of progress. It is itself a great creator of wealth. In 1929, for instance, the automobile manufacturer took in about $3,700,000,000. The total value of all manufactured products for that year was about $70,000,000,000. The value of the 1929 automobile was therefore equal to about 5% of the value of all manufactured goods. If we consider not only the auto manufacturer but also the auto body and auto parts manufacturer — that is, if we count not only Ford Motor Co. but also Briggs Mfg. Co. (bodies) and Kelsey-Hayes Co.

---

* It has over 375,000 stockholders; but E. I. du Pont de Nemours collects almost one-quarter of its dividends.

(wheels) — we find that the auto industry, in this larger sense, employed in 1929 about 450,000 wage earners whose wages came to $730,000,000. About 5% of the wage earners in manufacturing worked for the auto industry, and they collected about 6% of total manufacturing wages. You might say that the auto industry was about one twentieth of all American industry.

But in a broader sense it was a great deal more than that. The railroad industry, for example, took in nearly twice as much money as the auto industry, employed more than three times as many men, had almost four times the auto payroll. But the railroads did not make nearly as great a contribution to the national wealth. For the auto created a tremendous number of what might be called *derivative* jobs and generated a tremendous volume of *derivative* wealth. In 1929 there were nearly a million trucks on American highways. For a million trucks there were (at least) a million truck drivers. Add to this number some 600,000 chauffeurs. None of these men were on the auto maker's payroll; nevertheless the auto maker unquestionably created their jobs. There were also some 70,000 auto and accessory dealers, 120,000 filling stations and 65,000 garages. The Association of Automobile Manufacturers claim that over 950,-000 men were occupied in these branches of distributing and servicing automobiles — over twice the number of men engaged in the business of making automobiles. Add to these the enormous number of men employed in building and maintaining motor highways, and derivative jobs from the materials and services supplied to them, and a further picture of the real importance of the industry emerges.

Furthermore, the auto industry was one of the greatest customers of all other industries. It used more steel than the railroad industry or the building industry; indeed, the output of steel fluctuates almost precisely with the output of automobiles. It was the greatest single user of rubber, plate glass, nickel, lead, and was one of the top consumers of many other basic raw materials like copper and aluminum. One of its by-product industries, moreover, makes more money than the auto industry itself. The reference is of course to the petroleum industry, which exists primarily to sell gasoline. In years such as the present, when it is difficult to sell automobiles but when some 26,000,000 gasoline-devourers clog the highways, I should say that the petroleum companies would make several times as much as the motor car companies. Which, as far as I know, is the only case of an industrial offspring which has outstripped its parent.

It is, therefore, no wonder that the automobile is the industrialist's favorite child. And yet, as we know, few industries showed a heavier depression mortality. Between 1930 and 1935 almost the entire "independent" section of the industry went into a receivership or stopped producing altogether. And although it was the automobile that took the lead in the 1936–1937 "recovery", it was also the automobile that led the "recession" at the end of the year. Industry can no longer rely upon the motor car to move along at the head of its parade, yet so much of industry has fallen in line behind the automobile that when the motor car breaks down the whole procession comes to a standstill. The U. S. Steel Corp., which made $65,000,000 in the first six months of 1937, lost $6,000,000 in the first six months of 1938. Major cause of the difference was the fact that auto output for the first half of 1938 was less than 50% of auto output in 1937's first six months. As these lines are being written, the auto industry is getting ready to show its new (1940) models, most of which are sharply reduced in price. So auto sales for the coming season may be good. But I doubt whether it will ever again be possible for the auto business to effect a recovery in the sense of having two or three consecutive four-million or five-million car years. Yet a bad year for the auto industry is, to all practical purposes, a bad year for industry as a whole.

The economic woes of the present are sometimes referred to in terms of *overproduction* and sometimes in terms of *underconsumption*. Generally speaking, the expressions are no more than opposite sides of the same coin, although the second is usually preferable. For when you talk of overproduction, someone is certain to confuse production for use with production for profit and object that there can be no overproduction of, for instance, shoes until everyone has as many shoes as he needs or wants. Underconsumption avoids this confusion by putting the accent where it belongs — not on the producer's ability to produce but upon the consumer's inability to buy. And most of our industries today are suffering strictly from an underconsumption problem; the people want to wear more clothes and eat more meat and see more movies, but they lack the purchasing power to fulfill their needs and desires. Industries which manufacture consumer goods can almost always attribute their troubles not to the satiation of the customer's desire but to the emptiness of the customer's purse.

There is, however, one type of industry manufacturing consumer goods which may have an overproduction as well as an underconsumption problem. That is an industry which turns out consumer goods which last for a long time. The radio business is a very good illustration. There were more than 20,000,000 radio sets in use in this country as long ago as 1929 and since 1929 the radio industry has struggled, not very successfully, with a dual problem. There are a great many people who have no radio sets, who would like to have them, but who lack the money to pay for them. That, of course, is an underconsumption problem. But there are also a great many people who have the money to pay for a radio but who already possess one atmosphere-disturber apiece and are not on the market for more. This is a problem in overproduction for, even from a production-for-use standpoint, the radio industry could hardly expect to produce for these people. Already owning a radio, they *have no use* for another. All manufacturers of what are technically known by the title of "durable consumer's goods" run into this problem. Their market is limited by the price of their product and by the purchasing power of the people. They then proceed to oversaturate this market by producing more goods than the people in it can use. And, with the mass production facilities of modern industry, a very considerable market can be saturated in a very short time. It took the radio industry only about seven years to run into its first major setback. The electric refrigerator hardly got into mass production before 1927, but mass producers of the iceless ice-chest also consider that most of the families who could be considered likely prospects for electric refrigerators already have them.

I have gone through a rather long introduction to this overproduction-with-underconsumption problem because the automobile is the classic example of it. If, for convenience, we date the automobile from 1900, we may say that it took the auto maker some 23 years to saturate his market. For not until 1923 did the automobile manufacturers of the country produce more cars than their dealers could sell. Up to around that time — allowing for war-time interruptions and for the panic of 1921 — automobile factories ran practically at capacity. And at an enormously profitable capacity too. From 1904 to 1914 the Ford Motor Co. made 100% on its capitalization *every year;* that is, every dollar put into the business yielded a dollar's profit every twelve months even though a great many new dollars were constantly going in. From 1923 on, however, the ability of the auto industry to turn out new cars exceeded the ability (or the desire) of the people to pay for them. Yet, after the 1924 drop in production, the industry continued to make and sell more and more cars, and to take in more and more money. Auto production, by cars, from 1925 through 1929, was:

1925...................... 4,430,000
1926...................... 4,505,000

```
1927..................3,580,000
1928..................4,600,000
1929..................5,620,000
```

Auto production, by dollar volume, for the same years, was:

```
1925..............$3,015,000,000
1926.............. 3,215,000,000
1927.............. 2,700,000,000
1928.............. 3,160,000,000
1929.............. 3,575,000,000
```

In five years the industry had produced 22,725,000 automobiles at a manufacturer's value of $15,665,-000,000. (The retail price was in the neighborhood of $20,000,000,000.) But although 22,725,000 new autos were sold during this period, it is obvious that they were not sold to 22,725,000 new auto buyers. Most of them were sold to people who already had cars. To be precise, out of every 100 cars sold in 1929, no less than 72 were sold to purchasers who were already car-owners. This feat was made possible by the use of two selling devices – installment buying and the trade-in. Before discussing them, however, I should like to go back to the tables for a moment to discuss the pronounced dip in 1927 as well as the pronounced bulge in 1929.

The drop in auto production from 1926 to 1927

was about a million cars. Most of this decline was accounted for by the fact that the Ford plant was shut down during the greater part of this year. The famous old Model T, the "tin Lizzie" that Ford had been turning out unchanged for many years, suddenly dropped dead. In 1927, for the first time since Ford had got into mass production with his low priced car, the Ford failed to be the No. 1 selling car in the United States. It was supplanted by General Motors' Chevrolet. There were several reasons for this change. In the first place, Mr. Ford had made the mistake of losing William Knudsen, who promptly went over to General Motors and gave the Chevrolet (which badly needed it) the benefit of his skill and training. In the second place, General Motors, realizing that high priced cars were becoming more difficult to sell, concentrated their attention on the Chevrolet, their lowest-priced model, rather than on their Buick and Cadillac. (Walter Chrysler shifted his main effort from the Chrysler to the Plymouth in 1931 and gave Mr. Ford another terrible jolt.) But, in a broader sense, the collapse of the Model T showed the extent to which the auto business had become a question of *salesmanship*, not of *production*.

Mr. Ford was always a good producer. His Model T that did not sell in 1927 was just as good as the Model T that did sell in 1926. But Mr. Ford was a mediocre salesman. He was the man who said that the yearly model (i.e., a supposedly different car every season) was the curse of the auto industry. He was the man who didn't believe in advertising. He was the man who said that the public could have cars of any color it wanted, as long as it wanted black. Now from a production standpoint, all these remarks make plenty of sense, but from a selling standpoint they do not make any sense at all and the last one is little short of blasphemous. Yet Mr. Ford had been cheerfully ignoring his customers for many years, and with the greatest success. His car sold itself. Now it had to *be* sold. For the old days were gone forever.

The Ford shutdown in 1927 is also partly responsible for the final upswing in 1929. For while Mr. Ford was temporarily on the shelf, other auto manufacturers enlarged their plant-capacities to fill the gap. There was a possibility that Model T's successor would be no more popular than Model T, in its last stages, had been. At any rate, no one could tell how long it would take Ford to come back. As it turned out, Mr. Ford came back very successfully in 1928 and by 1929 was as good as ever. He advertised, he announced seasonal changes, and his cars had the colors of a rainbow. But the other manufacturers could not afford to let their unused capacity stand idle and they all came galloping down the 1929 stretch in what turned out to be the grand finale of the big prosperity revue. If Mr. Ford had only stayed out of business when General Motors put him out of business, the boom might have held on for another year. Not of course, that it would have made any difference in the long run.

To return, then, to the more serious matters of installment buying and trade-ins. Both were devices to make purchasing painless, but I can never see installment buying as the evil it is often said to be. Even in the worst years of the depression, the auto installment people did not have to "repossess" more than 6% of the cars they sold on time; the theory of a public with a future hopelessly mortgaged to installment payments overlooks the fact that the installment people are not in the business of extending blind credit. The trade-in, however, is an altogether different matter. For it was largely through the trade-in that the auto manufacturer was able not only to prolong the boom, but to prolong it at fancy prices.

On a low priced car, the dealer gets about a 25% markup — that is, if he pays the manufacturer $600 for a car, you get it for $750. The dealer has a $150 profit on the deal. But if you already are driving a car, you want the dealer to make you an allowance on it. Suppose that the dealer allows you

$125 on your used car. Now he has only a $25 profit, until he sells the used car. In his desire to make the sale, the dealer may have allowed you considerably more on your used car than he can get for it. Yet every dollar that he loses on the sale of the used car has to come out of his profit on the sale of the new car. Let us assume that the dealer gets rid of the used car for $100. He has made $150 on you but he has lost $25 on your car, so his profit is $125 on the deal. If this situation becomes general — that is, if all dealers are stuck with used cars on which they have to take a loss — the effect is that the dealer is taking what should have been the manufacturer's price cut. For if the manufacturer had taken $25 off the wholesale price of his car, the dealer would have had no loss on the trade-in. And since the dealer was forced to take the loss in order to make the sale, it follows that the car was $25 overpriced.

It is true that any retailer may discover that he has paid too much for what he has bought from a manufacturer, and is compelled to sell it at a markdown or bargain price. But the auto dealer has only one source of supply, his auto manufacturer. He is a Ford dealer or a Chevrolet dealer or a Plymouth dealer and he takes what Ford or Chevrolet or Plymouth sells him and tries to like it. If the automobiles are overpriced, the dealer in effect marks them down by making an overallowance on the trade in. We have already seen that General Motors made some $750,000,000 in the three years ending with 1929. I should very much like to know how much the General Motors dealers made during these same three years. We have also seen that General Motors made $435,000,000 in 1936-1937. I am quite certain that General Motors dealers made little if any profits during this period, particularly in 1937. For all year long the trade-ins were piling up on the dealers' hands, and used cars were glutting the used car market. Meanwhile the manufacturer was making more and more money and sending the dealer larger and larger quotas of overpriced merchandise.

I have gone a little ahead of my story in making this point about the trade-ins, but it is the central point in considering the question of why automobile production, instead of tapering off during the final years of the 1920's, continued to travel at higher and higher speeds until the inevitable crash was reached. You will remember that from about 1923 on the capacity of the auto plants was greater than the number of motor cars that the auto salesmen could sell. It therefore would be reasonable to expect that in the years following 1923 the production of automobiles would be gradually reduced, or would at most remain stationary. But the actual experience was a greatly increased auto production. In the six years ending with 1923, the auto maker turned out 14,000,000 units, or 2,300,000 a year. In the six years following 1923, he turned out 26,500,000 units, or 4,400,000 a year. He was, of course, assisted by the prosperity psychology of the period and by the fact that a good many hundred thousand individuals were going around with plenty of money in their pockets and with the firm conviction that there was plenty more where that came from. But he was also pouring more and more water into a jug that was already full, and he was making sales to persons who were spending tomorrow's income today. From the well-to-do stock market trader to the run-of-mine installment buyer, the nineteen twenty-niner was living on his anticipations. It was confidence in the future which had induced hundreds of thousands of car owners to trade in their cars every year or every other year for the sake of a shiny new model equipped with all the latest gadgets. As soon as that confidence had vanished, as soon as the crash in the stock market had signaled the end of the prosperity illusion, the auto maker found himself in a very bad way. During the period in which the foundations of his house were weakening, he had insisted upon climbing up to the roof. So when he fell, he had a long way to go.

In the five years following 1929 the auto-maker found himself compelled to curtail production, although his capacity, at the middle of the depression was somewhere between 7,000,000 and 9,000,-000 cars a year.* Here are the auto output figures from 1930 through 1934:

```
1930......................3,510,000
1931......................2,470,000
1932......................1,430,000
1933......................1,985,000
1934......................2,870,000
```

These figures show the characteristic down-swing, turning-point, and up-swing which mark what the economists call the economic cycle. Having produced "too many" cars (from the standpoint of the public's ability to buy them), the auto maker then produced "too few" cars (from the standpoint of his being able to make money on them) and by 1934 he was well back on the up-swing once more; that is, he was headed toward the point at which he would produce too many cars again. And, as we shall see in a moment, he again reached that point in a very short period.

There is, however, a weak spot in the theory that a period of overproduction can be "cured" by a

* According to Poor's Industry Service, 1933.

period of underproduction. If a man has been working too hard, or drinking too much, or otherwise exceeding his normal rate of operations, he may go off to the country or the seashore or a sanitarium and return with renewed ability to carry on. And, if his system has not been permanently impaired, he should be able to carry on successfully. For he comes back *to the same environment that he left.* He may be a new man but he has come back to his old world. For his period of inactivity did not interfere with the activity of anyone else.

It is not so, however, with industrial inactivity. *If* the curtailment of production meant *only* the curtailment of production, a period of low industrial output would indeed remedy the damage caused by a previous period of high industrial output. But what does the industrialist do when he cuts down production? He cuts down his payroll, too. Suggest to him that the only way to handle a period of bad business is to shut down on production but keep up on wages and he will consider you a lunatic. But of course when he cuts his payroll, he cuts the purchasing power of his community. And when all the industrialists cut all the payrolls, the purchasing power of the whole country experiences a very marked decline. Thus even his reduced output is still too great for the reduced purchasing power of his customers. The value of manufactures in 1929 was about $70,000,000,000. This output the public absorbed, although it broke its back doing it. The value of manufactures in 1933 was $31,000,000,000. But even this lowered dollar value was too great for the existing purchasing power, as is shown by the fact that in the spring of 1933 the entire economic system went to pieces and Mr. Roosevelt had to resort to all manner of artificial measures to put it together again. The industrialist (along with most orthodox economists) thinks in terms of production only. He must learn to think in terms of consumption as well. If the income of the people is reduced as rapidly as the output of industry, then the reduction of the output of industry can exert no influence in the way of bringing prosperity back.

This reasoning does not apply solely to the automobile industry, although the automobile industry is one of the best examples of the way it applies. We have said that, in 1929, the auto industry (including the auto parts industry) employed about 450,000 men to whom it paid wages of $730,000,000. In 1933, however, the industry employed 240,000 men and paid them wages of $250,000,000. The value of the automobiles and parts produced in 1933 was about 35% of the value of those produced in 1929. But the wages of the auto worker in 1933 were only 34% of what he had received in 1929. And of course the wages of workers do not have to decline very much to put them out of the auto-buying class. I do not wish to push this parallel too far, however — it is obvious that the auto maker does not depend upon the auto worker as his chief source of sales. But it so happened that the drop in the wages paid by the motor car manufacturer corresponded very closely to the drop in the value of the manufacturer's product, thus neatly illustrating the general trend of the times.

By the end of 1934, what with the N R A, the abolition of the gold standard, and the establishment of large scale Federal relief funds, the business world again seemed to be right side up. And the auto manufacturers were in a hurry to make up for lost time. In 1935 they stepped on the gas again, with the following production results:

```
1935.....................4,120,000
1936.....................4,615,000
1937.....................5,000,000
```

These records were extremely impressive while they were being made. The automobile was leading us out of the depression. We were in a recovery period, and the motor car had shown us the way. And indeed it did show the way to such measure of recovery as the country experienced. In the wake of increased auto output there was an increased output of copper, aluminum, nickel, glass, and particularly of steel. Long-closed factories were opened again. Long-idle workers went back to work. Long-unpaid bills were at least partially collected. And the administration was bitterly criticized for continuing "emergency measures" (i.e., relief payments and relief taxes) long after the "emergency" was over.

We now know, however, that the rejoicing was premature and the elation was short-lived. The stock market broke in the fall of 1937 exactly as it had broken in the fall of 1929 (and for the same reasons) and the industrial Jack and Jill went down the hill even more rapidly than they had gone up. Business had expanded too rapidly upon a purchasing power that was still not sufficiently restored. In September of 1937, just before the renewed collapse of the industrial world, unemployment, it is true, reached a post-1932 low — estimates ranged around 7,500,000. But these 7,500,000 unemployed constituted at least 15% of our total "employables." And against this background of diminished purchasing power, the industrialist was trying to operate at a rate which even the much greater purchasing power of 1929 had not been able to endure.

Here again the pattern of events is admirably illustrated by developments in the auto world. Here again the manufacturer succeeded in postponing the inevitable with the willing cooperation of the finance company and the less willing cooperation of the dealer. I have already admitted my blind spot on the subject of the installment-plan "evil," but in 1936 and 1937 auto financing was being conducted in such a manner as to disturb even those who had been well disposed toward it. In 1929 you paid for your car within a year, or at the most in 18 months. In 1936 and 1937 they were selling cars on time payments of 18 months, 24 months, and sometimes more. At the end of 1929, only 15% of installment paper (i.e., of the car buyers' notes on their cars) was more than one year old. But at the close of 1936, the notes not fully retired in 12 months amounted to 59% of the total. The British sometimes cynically refer to installment purchases as buying "on the never." We were at least getting into the position of buying on the long time from now.

But the trade-in was still the major problem and it was the trade-in that finally broke the camel's back. In 1929, you will remember, the dealer took a trade-in on 72% of his sales. By 1937, he was taking a trade-in on 88% of his sales. Furthermore, the problem of the trade-in *on the*

trade-in had arisen to add a final element of chaos
to the distribution of automobiles. It was not a
new problem, but in 1937 it had risen to new
heights. The trade-in on the trade-in appears when
the seller of a used car accepts another used car
to make his sale. It is a particularly vicious form
of barter for of course it leaves the used car seller
with another (and even longer-used) car to get rid
of. I have seen estimates that 50% of the people
who are now car drivers have *never* driven a new
car. This estimate sounds reasonable enough,
although I do not think its accuracy can actually
be checked.

Meanwhile the auto manufacturer was, for the
time being, coining money again. In 1937 General
Motors, even with the bad fourth quarter, paid
$170,000,000 in dividends — $3,500,000 *more* than
it had paid in 1929. Chrysler figures are not comparable, because Mr. Chrysler had not concentrated on the Plymouth in 1929, and Ford does not
take the public into his confidence as to what he
makes. But Packard was experiencing a marked
revival and several of the depression casualties
had staggered back into the arena and were re-
couping some portion of their depression loss.
Here again I should like to point out the conflict
between 43,000 auto dealers and (essentially)
three auto manufacturers. The dealer, the small

business man, takes the losses; the manufacturer, the big business man, takes the gains.

Eventually, to be sure, the realities of the situation caught up with the manufacturer himself. In November, 1937, he began to ship out his 1938 models. They were excellent automobiles but they carried a price close to 1929's. Furthermore, the stock market had already blown up, business was already going down, and an atmosphere of panic had succeeded the atmosphere of recovery. The dealer, knowing the condition of the used car market, could not possibly stand another flock of trade-ins. And the customers struck. The 1938 models piled up on the dealers' hands, and no amount of high pressure salesmanship could move them. The party was over and it was time for everybody to go home.

When the bad news finally filtered through Detroit's best minds, they reacted in a characteristic fashion. General Motors shut down its assembly line, fired 30,000 men, reduced its remaining 220,000 workers from a five-day to a three-day week. (Since the men work by the hour, this 40% time cut meant a 40% pay cut as well.) And thus the vicious circle of lowered production, lowered wages, still lower production, and still lower wages again started up. During the first six months of 1938 the automobile companies were running at less than 50% of their 1937 output. I should say it was safe to assume that payrolls had been at least correspondingly reduced. But I noticed that out of the wreckage of the recovery, General Motors had retrieved a $33,000,000 profit for the first six months of 1938.

The auto industry is a great monument to American individualism, although most of the individualists who were once in it are now dead. No one can go through the Ford plant at the River Rouge without conceding merit not only to the man who built it but also to the economic system which made his accomplishment possible. Yet the automobile industry has been a social failure because too few persons collected too great a portion of its profits, and because they pushed it along too rapidly in their attempt to collect more. If I think personally that Mr. Ford or Mr. Sloan or Mr. Chrysler makes too much money, my resentment may be ascribed to what someone has called "good, honest envy". But it is really not a question of anyone's making too much money; it is a question of so many people making too little money.

We have seen that, when the auto industry is busy, it employs about 450,000 wage-earners.

There are few harder jobs in industry – a man works in the midst of a mechanical jungle; the very movements of his arms and legs are determined not by him but by the pace of the machines around him. Yet even when the factories are busiest and work is most abundant he cannot reckon upon receiving more than about $35 a week. The least that industry should guarantee to such a man is security. It is not much of a job – industry should at least make it a safe job. It is not much of an income – industry should at least make it a steady income. The industrialist will say that he cannot guarantee these things without losing so much money that the investment in his property would be destroyed. This, with respect to the type of industry we are now discussing, is not true. It is true, however, that any form of guaranteed employment, although it would not destroy the investment, would undoubtedly reduce the return on it. But if what the industrialist says were true, there could be no more severe indictment of his system. For it amounts to saying that in order to preserve the riches of the rich it is necessary to perpetuate the poverty of the poor. From which, of course, arises the question as to whether the riches of the rich are worth their cost.

Chapter VIII

THE INVESTOR'S RETURN ON HIS INVESTMENT

ONE OF the reasons why the Main Streeter and the Wall Streeter so often fail to talk each other's language is the difference between their concepts of corporate profits. Most of us tend to think of profits in terms of absolute dollars — that is, we measure the profit in its number of dollars alone. We think that a company which makes $2,000,000 net income is doing twice as well as a company which makes $1,000,000 net. And when the profits run up into the multiple millions, our reaction is very pronounced. In 1937, for instance, the United States Steel Corp. made $95,-000,000. Some of us may consider this a great outrage and some may consider it a great achievement, but nearly all of us consider it great. In which, from the Wall Street standpoint, we are being naïve.

For Wall Street thinks of profits, not in terms of the number of dollars made, but in terms of the return on the capital invested. If a company should make $1,000,000 on an investment of $10,000,000, the financier would consider its earnings (he always refers to profits as *earnings*) very good indeed. For it would be "earning" 10% on the money invested in it. On the other hand, if a company should make $2,000,000 on an investment of $100,000,000, he would consider it a bad earner. For it would be making only 2% on its money. As for U. S. Steel's $95,000,000 in 1937, the Wall Streeter would be, perhaps, impressed but he would certainly not be overcome. For he knows that U. S. Steel is operating with an invested capital of about $1,600,000,-000, upon which the profit cited is a return of about 6%. So the Wall Streeter would say that "Big Steel" had a good, but by no means a miraculous, year.

Obviously there is an extremely wide divergence between the two points of view. The industrialist, indeed, usually dismisses all criticism of industrial profits on the ground that the critic does not know what he is talking about, because the critic often does not take into consideration this matter of the return on the investment. And whenever industry is convicted of following anti-social ways, apologists for the system as it is today, always fall back upon the investor's "right" to a return on his investment. Of course it is regrettable that factory wages never averaged better than $25 a week even in 1929. Indeed, it is unfortunate that unemployment reached 16,000,000 in 1932 and is in the neighborhood of 12,000,000 today. But, after all, the investor is entitled to a return on his investment. And even a profit of seven or eight billion dollars may be only three or four percent of the money the investor has put up.

Here, as always, the industrialist's spokesman lumps big business, little business, and medium-sized business together and of course has no difficulty in showing that the return on all the money invested in all business is very low. Indeed, in the first chapter we saw that since 1930 the net income of all companies has been a net deficit, so, on an over-all basis, industry has for some years been showing a minus return on its investment. At this point we are expected to become very sympathetic with "business" and very unsympathetic with the Administration and the C.I.O. and relief taxation and everything else that makes still more difficult the business man's hard lot. But we know, or we should know, that in these over-all figures the little man's losses are being used to disguise the big man's gains. Even if we are willing to discuss the matter of corporate profits solely in terms of the return on the investment (and, for reasons I shall point out below, we cannot accept the return on the investment as the sole criterion) we must at least insist on discussing the return on the big investment to the big investor by the big corporation in the form of big dividends. There is no point in arguing the profits of the International Harvester Co. with a man who insists on weighting them with the losses of a good many hundred corner drugstores. And it is the profits of companies like International Harvester (not of companies like the corner drugstore) that we may consider harmful to the general good.

There is also another matter of definition that we should insist upon before we get into any discussion of the investor's right to a return on his investment. Strictly speaking, no investor has any right to any return on any investment if by *right* he means (as he always does mean) that society is under an obligation to guarantee him a profit on his business. The investor himself, when he is not busy arguing about his *rights*, is even busier arguing about his *risks;* time and time again he advances the proposition that whatever profits he makes are justified by the immeasurable risks he takes in making them. But how can he have his rights and his risks too? The essence of any risk is the forfeiture of a corresponding right — if a man risks his life in a war he gives up whatever right he may otherwise have had to die a peaceful death. Who is more contemptuous than the industrialist of the *individual* who takes the attitude that the world owes him a living? Yet this is precisely what the big investor is claiming for himself.

The point here is of course that monopoly-industry, having virtually eliminated the element of business risk, is advancing quite a new argument about business rights. (I do not mean that the risk factor has been eliminated from every company, or even from every industry, but we have already seen that the 960 companies in the Standard Statistics sample averaged $380,000-a year profit even in 1932 and that their profits for 1937 were equal to their profits for 1927). If, however, the monopolist will stop talking about his risks we may be willing to discuss with him his "rights," always remembering, however, that this "rights" theory is directly contrary to the tenets of orthodox capitalism and really a distinct reflection upon American initiative, American individualism, and the good old American way. What we should perhaps concede is that the investor should have not the right but the *opportunity* to make a return on his investment. If, for instance, we should pass laws fixing the maximum price that he can put on his product, and if he could show that these prices *deprived him of the opportunity* of making a return on his investment, then he would be in a position to argue about his rights. He is, however, a long way from being in that position now.

That the industrialist himself feels a little conscience-stricken about his "rights" doctrine is shown by the fact that he usually couples the word "return" with the word "reasonable," and says he is entitled to a "reasonable return" on his investment. After all, no one would claim a right to an *unreasonable* return on an investment, so the qualification does not much clarify the problem. Furthermore, if we should incautiously agree that, say, 6% is a reasonable return on the investment, what happens when the capitalist doubles the investment? With twice the investment, he needs twice the profit to make the same rate of return. Perhaps he could make twice his original profit only by paying half his original wages. Then would he still be within the bounds of reason in holding out for his six percent? This whole idea of a right to a return or a right to a reasonable return on an investment is out of place except in a planned economy. If the government established reasonable wages for the worker and reasonable prices for the consumer, it should also be expected to establish reasonable returns for the investor. Under present conditions, however, the question of corporate profits cannot be settled merely by a reference to the investor's return on his capital. It is not realistic to judge corporate profits in terms of absolute dollars alone. But it is equally one sided to judge them solely from the standpoint of the return the investor would like to get, or has been used to getting, or from any similar point of view.

So let us turn from the consideration of what the big investor "ought" to get to a consideration of what he does get. (We shall, incidentally, find him doing very well even from his own return-on-investment point of view.) We shall not make much progress if we look at all the investors' returns on all their investments, for we know that on this basis the demonstration will merely show that the return is zero. On the other hand, no one company proves anything, for even among the large corporations there are the widest variations in the rate of return. In 1936, for instance, Eastman Kodak made 53% on its investment but the Pennsylvania Railroad made 4%. I have therefore taken a composite of 23 large companies as a representative section of big business.* (You will recognize them

* Namely:

General Motors	Texas Corp.
American Tel. & Tel.	Aluminum Co.
U. S. Steel	Sears, Roebuck
Du Pont	Reynolds Tobacco
Standard Oil (New Jersey)	Coca-Cola
Socony-Vacuum	Woolworth
Pennsylvania Railroad	Eastman Kodak
Anaconda Copper	Chrysler
Allied Chemical	Union Carbide
American Tobacco	General Electric
International Harvester	International Nickel
Bethlehem Steel	

from Chapter II.) For the sake of convenience, let us label the composite Industry, Inc., and look at some of its vital statistics in some of the critical years since 1925.

In 1925, when Mr. Coolidge had just been elected and when the United States had just become self-conscious but also self-confident about its prosperity, the twenty-three companies under consideration were in a highly prosperous state. They had capital stock of $5,950,000,000; a surplus of $2,750,000,000; and (therefore) capital and surplus of $8,700,000,000. Their total assets were $14,000,-000,000. Before we look at the return on this investment, let us see exactly what the figures mean.

The capital stock of a corporation represents the money (or capital) actually received by the corporation for its stock.* If Bethlehem Steel, for instance, offers 1,000,000 shares of stock to the so-called "public" at $50 a share, and gets $50,000,-000 for it, then Bethlehem has added $50,000,000 to its capital stock and has also added $50,000,000 to the amount of capital on which it attempts to make a return. The word capital stock is used to cover both common and preferred stock — the

---

* In the case of a no-par stock carried at a stated value, the company may have a capital surplus consisting of payments in excess of stated value.

dollar capitalization represents all the money actually paid in to the corporation by the investor. In the present case, the twenty-three companies had, over their various years of corporate life up to and including 1925, sold to the investor stock for which they had received $5,950,000,000.

The surplus of a company represents the accumulation of its undivided profits. That is, if a company makes $10,000,000 net income and pays out $7,000,000 in dividends, the remaining $3,000,-000 is added to its surplus. If for 20 years it makes each year $3,000,000 more than it distributes in the form of dividends, its surplus at the end of that period is $60,000,000.† In the case of the twenty-three companies, their accumulated undivided profits had grown, by 1925, to $2,750,000,000.

When we speak of a corporation's earning power, we usually consider the sum of the capital and the surplus as the amount on which the corporation earns. At first sight, this may seem unduly favorable to the investor because the return is figured on a good deal more money than he ever put into the concern. In the present case, for instance, the investor actually invested only about $5,950,000,-000 capital, but the capital and surplus comes to

---

† But the surplus is not kept around in the form of a cash balance, or reserve, or anything of that sort. A corporation spends its surplus as fast as it makes it, usually for plant expansion. It is nothing more tangible than the excess of the corporation's assets over its liabilities.

$8,700,000,000. But the investor, properly enough, figures that the surplus represents a part of his money which the corporation has held out on him. Sometimes stockholders are distinctly displeased by the amount of the profits that the corporation keeps for itself. Two of Henry Ford's stockholders (the Dodge Brothers) once got him into court and made him pay $19,000,000 of accumulated profits which Mr. Ford had been putting back into the business. That is why Mr. Ford bought out his stockholders and operates a strictly Ford family business today. Differences of opinion as to how much of the annual profits should remain undivided profits seldom reach such extremes, but it is always of both capital and surplus that the investor thinks when he thinks about the investment on which his corporations should be making a return. So the fundamental ratio in determining the corporation's return on its investment is the ratio between its net income and its capital and surplus. To show what the investor actually gets in dividends in return for the capital he has actually invested, however, I have also included the ratio of dividend payments to capital stock.

We see, then, that the 23 companies in 1925 had a capital of $5,950,000,000, a surplus of $2,750,000,000 and a capital and surplus of $8,700,000,000. What did they do in the way of a return on it?

They made $925,000,000 net income for the year. This profit is equal to 11% of the capital and surplus, and the rate of return on the invested capital was therefore 11%.

They were, however, stingy with their dividends. They were all expanding at a rapid rate and keeping as much as possible of their profits to spend on new plants and new machinery. So they paid only $485,000,000 in dividends. This amount came to 8% of the capital stock. The investor therefore realized only 8% on his actual investment. But he had the comforting assurance that his companies had retained about $440,000,000 to grow on, and that in subsequent years he should get bigger and better profits out of a bigger and better plant. To summarize, then, the companies made 11% on their investment; the stockholder got 8% in dividends on the capital stock.

Now let us look at these same companies in 1929. The first thing that strikes us is that the investment itself has tremendously increased. The 23 companies now have:

Capital Stock......... $8,000,000,000
Surplus.............. 3,800,000,000
Capital & Surplus......$11,900,000,000

The capital stock item is a little more than $2,000,-000,000 in excess of what it was in 1925 — an in-

crease of 36% in four years. Here is a really extraordinary expansion. Most of these companies
have had corporate lives of thirty or forty years.
Yet for every $1000 of stock that they sold in all
the years prior to 1925, they have evidently sold
another $360 of stock between 1925 and 1929.
Furthermore, the surplus has also mounted very
rapidly. It is $1,000,000,000 more than it was in
1925. The 1929 surplus is 38% larger than the 1925
surplus. So the undivided profits of these companies in the 1925–1929 period were equal to 38%
of their undivided profits for all their years up to
1925. And of course the capital-and-surplus figure
has also shown a marked growth. It has risen to
$11,900,000,000 – an increase of about 37% since
1925.

The significance of these figures is that the companies have to make a great deal larger dollar profit
in 1929 than in 1925 to show the same return on the
investment. They earned 11% in 1925 by making
$925,000,000; the same dollar profit in 1929 would
have given only an 8% return. Let us see, however,
what they actually did.

In 1929 the 23 companies made $1,600,000,000.
They needed a 40% increase over 1925 profits to
maintain their 1925 return on their investment.
But they actually got a 78% increase in profit.
And they made 13% on their investment – 2% more

than they had made on their much smaller investment of 1925. They were also a little more generous
with their dividends, paying to their stockholders
$925,000,000. Their 1929 dividend payments were
almost double their 1925 dividend payments. But
the investors had put another three billion dollars
into the concerns. Yet the investors, like the corporations, got an increased return on their increased investment, the ratio of dividends to
capital stock being 11%.

So the corporations made 13% on their investment and the stockholder got 11% on his stock.

(It may be noticed, incidentally, that in 1929
these 23 companies paid one-sixth of all the dividends paid to individuals by all the corporations
and that their net income was equal to about 18%
of the net income of all corporations.)

Now let us look at these same companies in 1932,
the last year of Mr. Hoover and the worst year of
the depression. There were 16,000,000 jobless in
1932; prosperity had long since vanished and panic
was very close. But these companies showed little
evidence of having gone through the worst three
years that American industry had ever known. In
1932 their vital statistics were:

Capital Stock......... $9,000,000,000
Surplus............... 3,000,000,000
Capital & Surplus......$12,000,000,000

Depression and all, the companies have sold nearly $1,000,000,000 more stock – the stockholders' investment is even bigger than it was in 1929. The surplus has indeed declined, through the payment of unearned dividends, but the decline in surplus is a little smaller than the increase in capital stock. And the capital-and-surplus figure is about a hundred million dollars greater than it was in 1929 – an increase, to be sure, of less than 1%, but an increase nevertheless. Theoretically, a depression is accompanied by a liquidation of capital; some companies go into bankruptcy or receivership, others exhaust their surplus attempting to meet dividend payments, none is expected to add to its investment by marketing further securities. But the 23 companies have not liquidated at all. They are all eminently solvent, most of them are still making money,* and their invested capital is greater than ever before. Their return on it, however, undoubtedly does show a depression influence.

In 1932 the companies made $200,000,000, which was a 1.7% return on capital and surplus.

But in 1932 they treated the stockholders very generously indeed. For they paid $555,000,000 in

* The big loser was U. S. Steel, which dropped $71,200,000 in 1932 and aided materially in bringing the profits of the 23 down to a decently low figure.

dividends. And this came to 6% of the stockholder's actual investment in the concerns. Having received 8% in 1925 and 11% in 1929, he still got 6% in 1932. Considering the state of the nation in general, I should say that the stockholder's return on his money was nothing about which to complain. Particularly since the national payroll for that year (all wages and all salaries) was about $31,000,-000,000 as against about $51,000,000,000 in 1929.

Now let us take a final look at these companies and see how they stood in 1936. Mr. Roosevelt had succeeded Mr. Hoover (at the close of 1936 he had just been reelected, much to the 23 companies' disgust), and every one was so sure that we had "recovered" that the big companies were starting off on their gallop into another collapse. We should expect to find the 23 companies in much happier conditions and our expectations are fully realized. For their 1936 figures were:

```
Capital Stock.......... $8,600,000,000
Surplus...............   3,000,000,000
Capital & Surplus......$11,600,000,000
```

The surplus has remained the same and the capital stock has somewhat declined (some of the companies having used recovery earnings to retire part of their preferred stock), leaving the capital and surplus much as it was before. The return, however, has shown an astonishing improvement.

In 1936 the companies made $1,220,000,000, which was 10% return on capital and surplus. This return was only about 10% less than the return on the investment in 1925 and was equal to nearly 80% of the return on the investment in 1929.

Furthermore, the companies were trying hard to make up for whatever dividends they had passed during their low-earning period. In 1936 they paid dividends of $960,000,000 — $35,000,000 *more* in dividends than they had paid in 1929. The ratio of dividends to capital stock was 11%, equalling the ratio established in 1929.

In comparison with 1925 — a good year for business as a whole; indeed, the year in which Coolidge Prosperity was just getting under way — the 23 companies:

Made $300,000,000 more profit, an increase of 32%

Paid $457,000,000 more in dividends, an increase of 98%

Increased surplus by $250,000,000, or 9%

Increased capital stock by $2,750,000,000, or 46%

Yet, with their capital intact and the major portion of their profits restored, they did nothing but complain about high taxes, extravagant relief expenditures, unbalanced budgets, rampant labor, pernicious radicals, and a hostile Administration that made it almost impossible for the business man to turn an honest penny as the reward of his hard day's toil. Today, with corporate profits again in a shrunken state, their complaints are even more bitter, their hostility even more pronounced.

There is an economic principle known as the law of the falling rate of profit. In its most general terms, it says that as an investment approaches infinity as a limit, the return on it must approach zero as a limit. Presumably no investment ever even approaches infinity as a limit, although the total assets of American Telephone are in the neighborhood of $5,000,000,000. And certainly, as the small investor has good reason to know, it is quite possible for the return on an investment not only to approach zero, but also to reach and pass it. A more everyday statement of the law, however, would be that as the investment in industry increases, the return on it tends to decrease. If we look at all industry in this country we shall see that the law already applies. The assets of all corporations in 1925 were about 150 billion dollars. The net income of all corporations in 1925 was about 7.6 billion dollars. Industry therefore earned about

5% on its assets. In 1929, however, the assets of all corporations were 335 billion dollars. The assets had more than doubled in four years. The 1929 net income of all corporations was 8.7 billion dollars. This net income was more than a billion dollars increase over the earlier year. But the asset-value had increased so enormously that the return on it was only 2.5%. And in the years following 1929, industry has either made no return upon its investment, or made a return so small as to be hardly worth the calculation. The assets of all industry dropped to 265 billion in 1933, a painful but salutary decrease. By 1934, however, they were back up to 300 billion dollars and in all probability they are well over that figure today. I am afraid that industry as a whole will never show an appreciable return upon such a valuation. Thousands of individual companies will of course make money and the total income of the profit-makers only may be a respectable percentage of the capital invested in them. But as far as the net income of all companies and the total assets of all companies are concerned, I do not see how industry will ever get more than the top of its head above water again. Which emphasizes the contrast between the situation of the many corporations and that of the few.

But why is it more difficult to maintain the rate of return on an investment as the investment increases in size? Because if you double your capitalization, you have to double your profits to make even the same return on your investment as you made before. Suppose that a steel company has an investment of $100,000,000 and it sells $75,000,000 worth of steel a year. This dollar volume is reached by selling 1,500,000 tons of finished steel products at an average price of $50 a ton. Allow the company 10 cents profit on every dollar of sales – a high but not an unheard of ratio – and it makes $7,500,000 for the year. Notice that the 10% return on the sales is only a $7\frac{1}{2}$% return on the investment. Nevertheless, the steel company is doing very well.

It is doing so well, indeed, that it can easily raise large amounts of new capital by issuing new stock. Let us suppose that it does go into the market for more money and that its total investment doubles to $200,000,000. Now, in order to maintain the same rate of return ($7\frac{1}{2}$%) on its investment, it will have to make twice as much profit. It will have to sell at least $1\frac{1}{2}$ times as much steel as it sold before. And with regard to the return on its investment, even a doubled profit represents merely holding its own.

But, it will be argued, we have just seen that the 23 companies, much as they increased their investment between 1925 and 1929, increased their profits even more. Nor would they have been able to increase their profits if they had not increased their investment. For it was the new capital which enabled them to expand their capacity and thus to produce more goods and make more money. This argument is entirely correct, and from it may be drawn the conclusion that a corporation can keep ahead of its rate of falling profit as long as its market expands more rapidly than its investment increases.

When, however, we are thinking of all companies and of all industry, the market becomes the purchasing power of the entire country. And when the investment in industry expands more rapidly than the purchasing power of the country, it is evident that the sales cannot increase in the same proportion as the investment. That industry, in the 1925–1929 period, did expand more rapidly than the expansion in purchasing power hardly requires an argument. In these five years, the investor bought no less than $28,000,000,000 of new corporate stocks and bonds. That meant a 28 billion dollar increase in the capital of corporations. During the same years, the undivided profits of corporations increased by nearly $11,000,000,000. That meant a 39 billion dollar increase in capital and surplus. Industry had therefore about $39,000,000,000 of new money on which to make a return.

Yet during the same years there was very little increase in purchasing power. There was a large increase in national income, but a very great percentage of this money was going to persons who were already wealthy and who used their surplus cash, not to buy consumer goods, but to buy more securities and thus to increase industry's capitalization. But it is the purchasing power of the masses on which the mass producer must rely. It is only the poor who have enough feet to absorb the output of shoes. And the purchasing power of the masses was increasing very slowly, while the investment in industry and the output of industry was rising at a rapid pace. Eventually industry discovered that it had solved the problem of mass production only to create a much more difficult problem of mass sales. Even in 1929 the industrial plant was not being run at its full capacity, for the industrialist knew that he could not dispose of a capacity output at a profitable price. And after 1929, although mass purchasing power dropped very rapidly (we have seen that the 1932 payroll was only about 60% the payroll of 1929) large industry, at least, retained nearly all its assets, nearly all its capacity, and nearly all its investment.

From 1933 through 1936 the purchasing power of the people moved gradually upward. Industry as a whole — or perhaps it would be better to say *competitive* industry as a whole — was still unable to show any appreciable return on its investment. Monopoly industry avoided deficits even in the worst of the depression years and, as we have seen, had restored the return on its investment to a level which would have been considered satisfactory in 1925. It did not, however, succeed in reaching its 1929 peak. In 1937, in a hurry to duplicate its 1929 earnings, it again turned on the full force of its productive plant. But the purchasing power of the public was again unable to absorb this output, and the result of the experiment was another rapid increase in unemployment and another spell of acutely hard times. The public was still only convalescing from its economic ailment and industry should not have asked it to take up its bed and walk.

And now even the monopoly capitalist is in something of a predicament. In 1938 he got what he considered a most unsatisfactory return on his investment. (And the competitive capitalist had another very large deficit to report.) The monopoly capitalist, in the latter part of the Big Boom, accumulated capital at a reckless rate. He was in an expanding market which he thought would expand forever. But it stopped expanding in 1929 and although it has since been subject to many fluctuations it has never re-attained its 1929 top. The monopoly capitalist makes sure that it never will get back to this level, for whenever he feels the pinch of circumstance he liquidates his labor instead of liquidating his capital.

In 1929 the capitalist knew that his investment had expanded beyond his market — he was holding back some of his potential output to let the market catch up. But the depression upset his calculations, and his system has never been self-operating since. That, incidentally, is why he has not been getting any new capital since the depression. Capital has been staying out of industry (and going into Treasury bonds) not because the President has undermined the investor's confidence in industry, but because industry has undermined confidence in itself. The industrialist cries for new capital, but what would he do with new capital except create more capacity that he could not use, except produce more output that he could not sell? This is the predicament in which even monopoly capital now finds itself. New capital would enable it to put on a temporary revival but it already has more capital than — from the standpoint of the investor's return on his investment — it can profitably employ. Even the large corporation is now threatened by a law that the Supreme Court cannot pass on and that even a Republican Administration could not repeal. The investor's "right" to what he considers a reasonable return on his investment has come into conflict with the fact that an investment cannot be forever increased with the rate of return on it being forever maintained.

Chapter IX

NOT ENOUGH LEFT

IN JUNE of 1938 the New York Stock Exchange took a sudden upswing, accompanied not only by rising prices but by a heavy volume of trading. One broker, who had already served forty of his clerks with dismissal notices, countermanded the order and kept them all on. On June 29, with a 2,658,000, share turnover, the market closed at the highest point reached since November, 1937.

There was almost nothing in the way of increased business activity to justify the return of a sensationally enthusiastic bull market. Steel mills were running at 28% of capacity, a figure which meant large deficits all around. Auto production was less than 50% of the production in the corresponding 1937 months, and there seemed little likelihood of any auto revival during the remainder of 1938. The United States Steel Corp. had just announced a sharp cut in steel prices. This move, in itself, was decidedly constructive and well calculated to stimulate trade. But from the Wall St. standpoint any

• 187

price cut is bad news, for the speculator does not bother about any long-term considerations and to him lower prices and lower profits are precisely the same. Corporation reports for the first three months of 1938 had been bad and forthcoming reports for the first six months were expected to be worse. Having failed to put on any spring revival, business was expected to relapse into its customary summer slump. And, under ordinary conditions, the market should presumably have been relapsing with it.

But although the stock trader does not look very far into the future, he does look beyond the present week or the present month. The speculator is not much interested in what a corporation made in the last quarter. To him, past profits, or losses, are only quotations already over the ticker. But he is very much interested in what a corporation may make in the next quarter and in the quarter after that. The market operates on the basis of anticipating future earnings or discounting future losses. In 1937, for instance, it reached its high for the year in March. By the time that the ordinary citizen had begun to think that recovery was certain, the trader had grasped the fact that the recovery was over. Hence the market went off in April and May, marked time during the summer, and took a nose dive in September, being by that

time thoroughly aware of the fact that high output, high prices, and high profits could no longer
be sustained. The June, 1938, market was therefore not responding to business conditions as they
were in June. It was responding to business conditions as the market hoped they might be during the
coming fall.

But if the present of business was so bad, what
made the future of business look so good? Chiefly
the feeling along Wall Street that industry, particularly the monopoly industry with which Wall
Street's attention is almost exclusively engaged,
was about to embark on a widespread and basic
campaign of wage-cutting. There were very excellent foundations for this suspicion. The railroads
had already "requested" the railroad unions to
accept a 15% wage cut. The unions objected violently to this proposition and the possibility of a
railroad strike was being widely discussed. The
Wall Streeter believed, however, that the Railroad
Brotherhoods would rather compromise on the
pay cut than risk a strike on the railroads, and that
if a strike did take place it would be easy to arouse
public opinion against it. (The possibility that the
railroad bondholders might take a 15% cut in the
interest on the bonds was, of course, not even suggested, the investor's "right" to the full return on
his investment being assumed to be more im-

portant than the engineer's right to his pay.) And if, by hook or by crook, a substantial wage cut could be put over on the Railroad Brotherhoods, the signal would be given for a concerted attack on union wages all along the line.

If this attack proved successful, the corporations would benefit in two ways. In the first place, by reducing their payrolls they would, for the time being, improve their profits. In the second place, a successful drive on union wage scales would be a serious set-back to the entire labor-union movement. It would be more difficult for the unions to increase their membership, more difficult to collect dues from members, and extremely difficult to carry any major strike to a favorable settlement. For a long time the Wall Streeter had been looking for a showdown between the big corporations and the unions, particularly the C.I.O. unions which showed such reluctance toward rolling over and playing dead when they heard the boss's voice. Now the action of the railroads had brought the situation to a head. Hence the sudden enthusiasm for the securities of U. S. corporations and the bull market which seemed to be moving upward without any visible means of support.*

* Contributing but subsidiary factors in the upswing were the resumption of the pump-priming effort at Washington and the rumors of another change in the gold content of the dollar.

A good illustration of the reasoning behind the market's bull movement was furnished by its reaction to the news that the United States Steel Corp. was cutting prices without cutting wages. This announcement was particularly shocking because it was timed to coincide with President Roosevelt's "fireside chat" of June 24, in the course of which the President, obviously referring to U. S. Steel's price cut (which he thoroughly approved), added that he "understood" that the price cut would not be followed by a wage cut. The Steel Corporation's announcement, plus the President's "understanding," gave the market considerable pause. On the morning after the price cut, the corporation was swamped with telegrams (legitimate telegrams) the gist of which was "Say it isn't true, Eddie,* say it isn't true." And not only U. S. Steel stock slumped when the stock market opened; there was a downward movement along the entire list of the selected stocks which formed the basis for the bull movement. If the corporations intended to cut prices, instead of wages, the stock trader wanted no part of them.

Reassurance was, however, prompt. The U. S. Steel Corp. said that its price cut should be considered apart from its wage-rates, that there had

* Edward Stettinius, Jr., who, as we have mentioned, had succeeded Myron Taylor, as No. 1 man at U. S. Steel.

been no promise to maintain wages, and that future wages were dependent upon future conditions of business. Nobody said anything about Mr. Roosevelt's "understanding," but there was a very strong implication that whoever was responsible for it had at best been talking out of turn. The Street promptly concluded that Big Steel had announced its price cut to pave the way for future wage cuts. This cynical interpretation may have been entirely unfounded, but it was certainly the interpretation on which the market acted. For after having heard from U. S. Steel, the market instantly resumed its rise. A few days later Mr. Ernest Weir, the white haired boy of the steel industry until he surrendered that honor to Tom Girdler, issued a statement deploring the price reduction and indicating that it would have a very bad effect on the state of steel. Happier than ever, the Wall Streeter decided that even if the U. S. Steel Corp. should attempt to maintain wage scales, the Girdler-Weir-Grace section of the industry would undoubtedly cut its wages as a result of having to meet U. S. Steel's prices. So the boom boomed higher than ever and the general public was puzzled by the apparently odd coincidence of industry proclaiming that the wolf was at the door while the stock market was turning in new highs every day.

The philosophy of the stock market is also the philosophy of the large stockholder although the latter, with his life-long interest in the corporations, looks at things in a somewhat broader perspective. The speculator buys stock for a quick resale. The investor is interested in the dividend return over a long term. He is concerned not only with corporate earnings in 1938, but with corporate earnings in 1948 as well. Like the trader, he knows that a reduced payroll means an increased immediate profit. Unlike the trader, he has to look beyond the near future and think in terms of something approaching ultimate results. It should be difficult for him to look cheerfully ahead or to think happy thoughts about what lies before him.

To the more intelligent and more far-seeing capitalist, the course of events since 1929 — or even, in retrospect, since 1925 — must be profoundly disturbing. He knows that in 1929 his structure of prosperity collapsed of its own weight. There was no one then who pushed it over, no one then who undermined its strength. Furthermore, the conventional method of handling a depression — by doing nothing and letting it run its course — turned out disastrously. The system appeared to have lost its recuperative power. In 1932 it was repudiated by the people and in 1933 it repudiated itself. The panic was halted and an upswing brought about by measures which in 1929 the capitalist would have regarded as both destructive and insane. Yet despite the assistance given by the New Deal – and in 1933 and 1934 even the large investor conceded that the New Deal *was* an assistance – Humpty Dumpty, back on the wall, showed little ability to maintain his balance. It must be remembered that the essence of our present economic system is that it should operate *automatically*. The theory has been that, with every man for himself, there will still not be too many hindmost for the devil to take. The capitalist has never, in his more sober moments, claimed that the general good was among the objectives of his activities. But he has claimed that an unintentional but inescapable by-product of his success has been an improvement in the condition of the people as a whole. Hence, for example, the once-frequent references to the American standard of living, and the once-boastful citations of the number of automobiles, telephones, bathtubs, radios, and other personal possessions owned by the inhabitants of the United States. In 1929, when these references and these citations were most common and when the auto industry was actually attempting to convince the public that one car per family was not enough, the industrialist sincerely believed, I think, that prosperity for him was prosperity for everyone. His thinking was superficial and he kept his eyes away from the darker side of his prosperity picture. But he was probably not fooling the public so much as he was fooling himself.

And now it is hardly possible for him to fool himself any longer, although for that very reason the necessity of fooling the public is greater than ever before. The large investor must have at least begun to realize that it is no longer a question of his prosperity *and* the public's prosperity but of his prosperity *or* the public's prosperity. If he needed any final demonstration of this proposition, the failure of his 1937 recovery should have supplied him with it. During the first five months of 1937 the basic producing industries — the metal, mining, fabricating, and mass-manufacturing industries which used to be his particular pride — were in many instances operating at close to 1929 rates of production and selling at close to or higher than 1929 prices. In April, 1937, for instance, the steel industry was operating at over 90% capacity, and it had made large increases in its capacity since 1929. Even for the full year, and with due allowance for the slow-down in the third quarter and the collapse in the final three months, the 1937 output of petroleum, aluminum, nickel and several other basic commodities was greater than the output of these commodities in 1929. And, as we saw in Chapter II, many corporate profits in 1937 were close to or more than the 1929 profits of the same concerns.

The stage was, therefore, set for a recovery. The public, indeed, thought that a recovery had taken place. So did the industrialist, but not for very long. The market, as I have said, lost the courage of its convictions in the spring, remained watchfully waiting throughout the summer, and let go in September when it saw that its worst apprehensions were being realized. And the large stockholder knew, even better than the market trader, how transient was his boom. In December, 1937, I read a report from some investment service or other which, with the professional optimism of nearly all investment services,* thought that possibly the "present depression was over," because it had *already had nine months* in which to run its course. Thus the "smart money" dates the "recession" not from September, 1937, but from March. Even if we date "recovery" from the closing months of 1936 — it was really getting under way

---

* People who sell advice about the stock market thrive in proportion to the number of persons who play the market. But the small trader, who makes up the bulk of the investment service's clients, almost always enters the market only when he thinks it is going up. Either he has not mastered the intricacies of the short sale or he is a congenital optimist. At any rate, investment services know that they will not attract customers by predicting that the market is going down. So they commonly look through rose colored glasses at the brightest side of things.

at about the time that Mr. Roosevelt buried Mr. Landon — it can hardly be said to have had more than a five months' life.

And, despite the outbursts of editorial writers and other small industrial fry, the large stockholder knows very well that the demise of the recovery cannot be attributed to the New Deal. It is true that in April, 1937, the President warned the industrialist that he was overproducing and overpricing. The President was perfectly correct in his statement, but the argument that the subsequent fall in prices and production was caused by it is ridiculous indeed. A good many statements have come out of the White House during the past eight years without having the slightest influence on industry's way of life. What happened was that overproduction was so great and prices were so high that customers refused to buy. Indeed, when the boom got down to the retailer (that is, when the large output of high-priced manufactured goods reached the man who had to sell them to the ultimate consumer), the boom was instantly over. The industrialist was trying to sell a 1929 production to a 1937 public. And with about 7,500,000 people still out of work, with such re-employment as there was concentrated in manufacturing industries alone, the purchasing power of the public was unable to support the burden put upon it. We have seen how the auto output of 1937 backed up on the manufacturer even before the end of the year. And early in 1938 radio dealers were dumping marked-down radios on the market, just as they dumped similarly marked-down radios on the market in the early months of 1930. The technique of 1937 was the technique of 1929. And it produced the same disastrous result.

Yet this was the only technique that the industrialist knew. The industrialist has a great capacity for making an advance but he is extremely awkward about beating a retreat. He is a natural expansionist, who grew up in an expanding economy and prospered on an expanding market. What left him so dazed in 1930 was the fact that he was going through a new experience. He had been through depressions before, but this one was evidently different. And the longer it lasted, the more perplexing it became. In 1937, for a few months, it seemed that the world had again turned right side up. But the appearances soon showed that they were deceptive. In the spring of 1938, industry was crawling along at such low levels that even professional optimists were being discouraged. Subsequently, with $1,400,000,000 of WPA money being put into circulation as rapidly as possible, business was somewhat improved. But again it was leaning heavily on the Administration and again it had demonstrated its inability to get anywhere by itself.

And so the industrialist and his stockholding partner are abandoning the idea of collecting boom-time profits and concentrating on the problem of collecting bad-time profits. And here is where they are becoming distinctly a menace to the general good. As we have already seen, it is not so difficult for the large corporation to make money. Except in periods of the most acute depression, it is not so difficult for the large corporation to make money even according to its own return-on-the-investment standard. In bad times, the income of the corporation contracts sharply. But so do its expenses. It reduces its payroll and it also reduces the money it spends on materials and supplies. In a large manufacturing company, wages may come to about 40% of production costs, with materials and supplies making up the 60% remainder. Partly because the corporation pays somewhat lower prices for its materials in bad times, but chiefly because it has so much less material to buy, it makes extremely large savings in its largest single item of expense. All of this may appear self-evident, but I do not think people generally realize the corporation's ability to diminish its outgo as rapidly as its income is diminished. Perhaps the best example of this shrinkage-capacity is shown by General

Motors' figures for 1929 and for 1932.

In 1929, General Motors took in $1,500,000,000 on sales.

It paid out $390,000,000 in wages and salaries.

It paid out roughly $770,000,000 for other items, including materials and supplies.

After meeting the cost of labor, the cost of materials and its other expenses it had about $340,000,000* left.

The 1932 figures are of course very different from those of 1929:

In 1932, General Motors took in $430,000,000 on sales.

It paid out $145,000,000 in wages and salaries.

It spent some $240,000,000 on materials, etc.

After meeting the cost of labor, materials, and its other expenses it had $45,000,000* left.

Now we can see more clearly the extent to which a corporation can pull in its horns when necessary. The auto company's 1932 sales were only 29% of its 1929 sales. But as its income declined, its expenditures declined as well. It took $245,000,000 off its payroll, leaving a 1932 cost of labor equal to 37% of its 1929 cost of labor. (This amounted to firing three-fifths of its 1929 workers.) It took about $530,000,000 off its other costs, this item

---

* These figures, as listed in General Motors income accounts include non-operating as well as operating profits.

standing in 1932 at 30% of its 1929 level. On the two items together it made savings of $775,000,000. And because of these economies it was able to pay a $63,000,000 dividend in 1932 with no appreciable damage to the large surplus it had accumulated in previous years.

General Motors is, of course, only one example of the corporations' ability to match contracted receipts with contracted expenditures. In 1929 the entire manufacturing industry (about 210,000 corporations) paid wages of $11,600,000,000 to 8,800,000 wage-earners. It also spent $38,-200,000,000 on materials and supplies. These two items come to approximately $50,000,000,000. In the same year, the manufacturer took in just under $70,000,000,000.

In 1933, however, the manufacturer paid wages of only $5,300,000,000 to only 6,000,000 men. Since 1929 he had reduced his labor cost by nearly six and one-half billion dollars. His 1933 cost of materials and supplies came to only $16,800,-000,000 — a decline of more than twenty billion dollars from 1929. Wage costs plus material costs were only twenty two billion dollars in 1933, compared to fifty billion in 1929. Which means that the manufacturer was paying out about twenty eight billion dollars less than he had paid out in the boom year. It is true that his income had also experienced a violent decline. He took in only about $31,300,000,000 in 1933 – a shrinkage of about $38,700,000,000 from 1929. His decline in income was about ten billion dollars greater than his savings in the cost of wages and materials, hence the large deficit which he accumulated for the year. We have already seen, however, that the biggest companies, as a unit, made no contribution to this deficit, that notwithstanding the decline in their incomes, they still retained a profit for the year.

The immediate point, however, is not the earning power of the companies, but their spending power. They put twenty eight billion dollars less money into circulation in 1933 than they had put into circulation in 1929. But although there were not as many job holders in 1933 as in 1929, there were just as many persons who wanted and needed jobs. In fact, since the population of the country was increasing, there were several millions more. At $1,000 a year, the money which the companies did not spend in 1933 would have supported 28,000,000 families. I am not saying that the companies could or should have spent the money. I am saying that an economy subject to such violent contractions is not an economy under which working-people (including the salaried and the self-employed) can count upon any reasonable degree of security in their lives. It should also be remembered that (as we saw in the previous chapters) the largest companies not only survived the Depression but came through it with capital, surplus and assets almost unimpaired.

The only type of large corporation whose corporate life a depression seriously menaces is the corporation with a large funded debt. The bondholder demands his interest, in good times or bad, and this expense is a fixed charge which the corporate manager cannot escape. Hence, the railroads, with their billions of dollars of bonded debt, wobble along on the edge of receivership in any sustained low-income period. The electric light and power companies also have accumulated a heavy load of bond interest. So far they have been able to carry it (because their position as "natural" monopolies keeps business always good), but in another fifteen or twenty years the utilities may find themselves in the same position that the railroads now occupy. The immediate point, however, is that the large manufacturing corporations (which have usually secured capital by selling stock, not bonds) have more lives than a cat. The investor's return on his investment is reduced, and sometimes interrupted. But his capital itself is in a place considerably safer than a bank.

This pleasant situation, however, is brought

about only by a stringent cost-cutting program on the corporate management's part. And cost cutting comes down primarily to wage cutting. In 1929, General Motors employed about 230,000 men. In 1932, it employed about 115,000. So it contributed 115,000 men to the ranks of the unemployed and subtracted $245,000,000 from purchasing power. The money it saved on materials and supplies also had much the same effect. It contributed to unemployment among the mining and fabricating companies which sell to General Motors. In its cost-reduction program, the auto company took $775,-000,000 off the buying power of the public. It is strange that, at the time of a strike, the sympathy of local merchants is usually with the employer. At such a time, the merchants have no difficulty in associating interrupted payrolls with interruptions in their trade. Yet when companies fire men and cut wages the effect is much the same and the reduction in payrolls lasts much longer than any strike. Yet the merchants do not seem much piqued at the companies. Perhaps it is a matter of class solidarity, although the small merchant's position as a capitalist is becoming more technical every day. At any rate, the employer during a depression is a very different person from the employer in a boom. He was, occasionally, a good fellow when he had it. But he is likely to be a bad fellow when he is trying to keep it or to get it back.

I may be attributing to reflection what is merely
a matter of instinct. The industrialist may not
have thought things over and decided that from
now on cost cutting must be the order of the day.
It may be that he has simply found himself, during
the past nine years, in a series of positions in which
the line of least resistance was to fire somebody,
and the line of least resistance is the line he always
takes. Yet, whether through intention or instinct,
his attitude has undeniably altered. Even when his
1937 boom was still booming and large profits were
being run up, he (for the most part) put up a stub-
born resistance to labor organization — a resistance which, in the case of the Little Steel strike,
resulted in many deaths. In 1929 he was, relatively
speaking, well disposed toward labor unions. Not
that he had much to worry about from any organization of which Mr. William Green was president.
Indeed, he liked to have Mr. Green speaking at his
conventions and dinners to show that Capital
could be broad-minded and Labor could be respectable. And of course Mr. Green did not try to organize the steel industry. Still, in the spring of 1937,
the steel industry was making plenty of money. Its
more enlightened branches (particularly the United
States Steel Corp., under the direction of Myron
Taylor and J. P. Morgan & Co.) had no difficulty in
coming to an agreement with the C.I.O. But its
more feudalistic sections (particularly the Republic

Steel Corp., under the direction of Tom Girdler) fought the C.I.O. with bombs and bullets. And, with the assistance of Martin Davey, then Governor of Ohio, although later defeated in an attempt to secure his party's renomination for that job, the Little Steel companies temporarily blocked the unionization of their plants.

Even in the best of times Mr. Girdler was a union-fighter, and while working for the Jones & Laughlin Steel Corp. in its plant at Aliquippa, Pa., he made Aliquippa extremely unsafe for industrial democracy. His job as head of Republic Steel, however, gave more scope to his natural talents and the C.I.O.'s attempt to organize Republic furnished a splendid example of a meeting between the man and the hour. And, sadly enough, the manner in which Mr. Girdler rose to the occasion was widely applauded by some of the more backward elements in our society and even more widely condoned by others. But I do not think he will ever be discussed as a presidential possibility except perhaps for the presidency of the American Iron and Steel Institute. To most of us, Mr. Girdler probably figures as the type of the bad industrialist. Yet Mr. Girdler is the product of depression, precisely as the "good" industrialist was the product of prosperity.

I think it is only upon the assumption that the industrialist has reconciled himself to operating in a contracting economy, but has not reconciled himself to operating with contracted profits, that many of his recent actions can be explained. When the 1937 recovery exploded, the industrialist instantly resorted to large-scale payroll cutting. American Federation of Labor figures show that from September, 1937, to January, 1938 close to 2,000,000 workers lost their jobs. And industrial unemployment grew by another two million in the first six months of the present year. The decline in employment was far greater than the decline in the closing months of 1929, catastrophic as those months were. Employment at the end of 1929 was less than 10% below peak employment for the year and held remarkably well for the first six months of 1930. By that time it had become apparent that Mr. Hoover and his friends could not talk the country out of a depression, and from then on unemployment increased at a rapid rate. In 1929 and in the first half of 1930 the industrialist was still prosperity minded. When he found himself confronted with a crisis, he did not know precisely how to act. But in 1937 he knew all about depressions. He had no hesitation about what to do. Instantly he cut down production, cut down his payroll, kept up his prices,* and went

---

* Steel billets sold for $37 a ton in April, 1937, with mills at 90% of capacity. Mills were at about 30% of capacity in March, 1938. Steel billets still sold for $37 a ton. The subsequent cut in steel prices has been mentioned above.

into his shell. The result was a revival of the depression in its most acute stages and a renewed necessity for the Administration to supply relief money and relief projects with which to bail the economic system out.

The industrialist's psychological reaction to October, 1937, is also an interesting contrast to his reaction to October, 1929. In the earlier period, although shocked, he remained optimistic. Even after his optimism had dwindled, he remained cheerful when interviewed by the press. After all, prosperity had been his baby, and he did not like to admit that he dropped it. Remember the bankers' pool formed in October, 1929, to prop up the stock market? At a time when graphs showing the course of stock-market quotations were heading for the bottom of the page in a perpendicular line, Richard Whitney, the pool's representative on the Exchange floor, melodramatically bid $207 a share for U. S. Steel and for some time Mr. Whitney figured as the Sir Galahad of the financial world. To be sure, the entire performance did not amount to much more than a drowning man's insisting that the water was fine, but it gave the banking heart the appearance of being in the right place. And in the spring of 1930, with Mr. Hoover insisting that a panic positively would not arrive, even the market rallied from its 1929 lows and the progress of depression was, for a little while, retarded.

In 1937, however, the industrialist was not interested in holding up the market or in minimizing the bad condition of the country's affairs. His interest, indeed, lay in precisely the opposite direction. For now not Mr. Hoover but Mr. Roosevelt was in office and the worse the depression could be made to look the more, perhaps, it could be made to look like Mr. Roosevelt's doing. The same oracles who were publicly engaged in making the best of everything in late 1929 and in 1930 were even more publicly engaged in making the worst of everything in late 1937 and in 1938. Nor did the bankers form any pool to support the market or nominate any hero to go through the motions of saving it. But the capitalists did not care about saving the 1937 market. After all, it was not their market to save.

As to a "strike of capital," however – in the sense of the capitalist deliberately attempting to ruin the economic structure in order to hold Mr. Roosevelt responsible for the crash – this point of view is, I think, more melodramatic than realistic. The investor is too fond of his dividends to bite them off, even to spite Mr. Roosevelt's face. He is certainly willing to lend his vocal support to any anti-Roosevelt measure, but it would be risky to rely upon him for too great tangible help. He did a good deal of talking for Mr. Hoover, but he also kept production low and unemployment high. He will do a great deal of talking against Mr. Roosevelt and he will make personal financial contributions to any anti-New Deal cause. But capital is not staying out of industry to discredit Mr. Roosevelt. New Capital is staying out of industry because the capitalist is afraid that industry cannot consistently make a satisfactory return on the capital already in its possession.

Between 1922 and 1929, the industrialist proceeded on the supposition that business would always be even better tomorrow than it was today. And, for the period in question, the supposition was justified by the facts. In that time the industrialist was figuratively as well as literally expansive: wages were steady, employment was regular, new jobs were created; on the surface, everything went well. But since 1929 even the large companies, as a group, have not duplicated 1929's production or 1929's profit. They can still make money, but not by their methods of ten years back. At that time they were most interested in creating wealth, now they are most interested in preserving it. They are even more mechanized today than they were in 1929 — that is, they can produce an even greater output with even fewer men. They are still taking their dividends out of the system and after they have taken out their dividends, there is not enough left. Particularly, there is not enough left for wages. And so the industrialist has to play rough.

Labor and capital can collaborate successfully only when the capitalist's market is increasing and the capitalist's profits are high. At other times, the lamb's willingness to lie down with the lion will not turn out well for the lamb. The industrialist today is not thinking of how to step up production. In every basic industry he already has far more capacity than he can profitably use. His interest is now in cost cutting. That is why, for instance, he thinks that the Wagner Act should be "amended." That is why he hates the National Labor Relations Board almost as wholeheartedly as he hates the C.I.O. That is why he wants a Republican administration to help him break strikes, to repeal the Social Security Act, to substitute sales taxes for income taxes, to "balance the budget" by economizing on relief. It is not only the worker who is threatened by this program, for it is a program that means a permanent depression for all except the few who are already secure. It will lead to a decline in the standard of living for all persons except those whose standards are already too high. In the long run, it is a dangerous program for the industrialist, for he cannot follow it and still argue that his interests are the interests of the community on which he lives. But the long run cannot engage too much of the industrialist's attention. He has his dividends to pay now.

Chapter X

THE FALSE FRONTS OF CAPITALISM

In THE autumn of 1932, just before the Roosevelt election, Montague Collet Norman, Governor of the Bank of England, made a speech to his fellow-bankers in London. Talking of the depression, Mr. Norman said, "The difficulties are so vast, the forces so unlimited . . . the whole subject . . . is too great for me." With this statement the high priest of capitalism conceded the collapse of his system; the medicine man admitted he had no more medicine to dispense.

From the standpoint of political-economic tactics, Mr. Norman's statement was more candid than discreet. It was a remark of the kind that always comes back to haunt its maker. Yet, at the time, no American banker or industrialist ventured to dispute it. Mr. Charles Mitchell, boom-time head of the National City Bank, was under a cloud. So was Mr. Albert Wiggin, boom-time head of the Chase National Bank. Mr. Insull was abroad. The Van Sweringens were wondering what was going to happen to their empire. Nobody was calling Andrew Mellon "the greatest secretary of the treasury since Alexander Hamilton". Wall Street was, for the time being, not only defeated but discredited. And in a moment when crisis was turning into panic, it did not have a word to say in its defence. The hat was empty now and no more rabbits would come out.

Yet from the Harding election in 1920 to the Roosevelt election in 1932 the industrialist had been completely in the saddle, supported by the politician and public alike. He had been in power for so long that it had become necessary to invent a philosophy for him, hence the slogans about "making everybody rich" and "a chicken in every pot." His political agent, the Republican party, had won three successive presidential elections with such ease that the Democratic party seemed likely to go out of existence as a serious competitor on a national scale. The industrialist conducted himself as if he had invented prosperity. And the public appeared willing to give him a patent on it.

It is amazing now to look back on the later 1920's and see how many false values were unquestioned, how many superficial reputations were built up. Calvin Coolidge, for example, was widely regarded as the typical American and the perfect President. As a matter of fact, Mr. Coolidge rode

into office on the disreputable coattails of Warren
Harding, and became President only because of
Mr. Harding's timely death. Toward the end of
his administration, it was often difficult to tell
whether Mr. Coolidge was imitating Will Rogers or
Will Rogers was imitating him. It is unfortunate
that Mr. Coolidge "did not choose" to run again in
1928. For there would have been an interesting
struggle between his Yankee wit on the one hand
and the depression on the other.

But as a moral lesson and a sorry object Mr.
Hoover serves nearly as well. As Secretary of
Commerce, he had been thoroughly identified with
Coolidge prosperity, and under few Presidents has
the alliance between business and politics been
more complete. It was on a prosperity platform
that he ran against Alfred Emanuel Smith, and
the prosperity issue was so persuasive that the
Brown Derby was beaten even in its home state.
Not that it would have made any difference if
Mr. Smith had won. The 1928 election was indeed
an excellent illustration of the fundamental identity of the two major parties. Hoover was dry and
Smith was wet. Hoover was (now, if not in the
beginning) a rich boy and Smith had at one time
been a poor boy. Hoover was a bad candidate and
Smith was a good candidate. But there was no
real conflict between them. Today, indeed, when

there is a very real issue between the Republicans and the Democrats, Al Smith is a Republican in everything but the name. He has even been given a niche in prosperity's big tombstone at Fifth Avenue and Thirty-fourth St.

Mr. Hoover has often said that he was not to blame for the depression, and the statement is entirely correct. He merely happened to be roosting in the prosperity tree when the lightning struck it and anyone else in the same position would have been felled by the same bolt. It is Mr. Hoover's conduct after the depression that is more open to criticism. For a long time he denied that there was any depression. Even when it occurred to him that something more significant than a flurry in Wall Street had happened, he would not insult the independence of any rugged American individualist by putting him on a dole or otherwise sapping his manhood and self respect. Possibly the theory was that a man's manhood flourishes when he is jobless and his self respect rises in proportion to the hunger of his children.

To be sure, Mr. Hoover made a considerable financial contribution to industry, particularly to the railroad industry. But then a railroad has no self-respect and the people who control its stock are usually most conspicuous for their self-esteem. Yet although Mr. Hoover muddled, he did not manage to muddle through. In 1932 the votes of the people retired him to private life from which, to the discomfort of the present Republican party leaders, he occasionally emerges in the form of a speech or trip.

One of the more interesting memories of Mr. Hoover is his excuse for the depression. He maintains that it was a world-wide depression and that America caught it from overseas. In disclaiming responsibility for the collapse of the profit system in this country, Mr. Hoover was merely advertising the collapse of the profit system in all countries. "Do not blame me," said Mr. Hoover, in effect, "because you are not prosperous. Nobody is prosperous in any capitalist country anywhere in the world."

In speaking of Mr. Hoover I have also been speaking of the entire group of bankers and industrialists whom Mr. Hoover represented so well. Like him, they at first could not believe that prosperity was over. The concept of many years of depression was too much for their bewildered minds to grasp. In 1930, for instance, they declared corporate dividends of about eight billion dollars, about 98% as much as they had declared in 1929. And corporations, you know, are supposed to save their money for a rainy day. (Remember the fuss they made about the undistributed profits tax because it would prevent them from accumulating a surplus on which to live in bad times?) The companies would never have been so generous with their stockholders if they had realized what lay before them. By the time they realized that the situation was critical, they also decided that the situation was hopeless. Today the usual industrialist hates the New Deal and all its works. In 1933, however, the badly frightened banker and industrialist was – for a very brief period – so well pleased at having been rescued from disaster that the identity of his rescuer and the manner of the rescue did not concern him.

We did not hear anything about regimentation or dictatorship in the New Deal's early days. But how could the traditional system of freely-functioning individual enterprise be more violently interfered with than by the "interference" of the Federal Government in 1933? The banker was forced to close his bank. The enterpreneur was forced to adopt uniform prices. Mr. Roosevelt even broke into the very ark of the tabernacle and impiously substituted the baloney dollar for the gold standard.

The early activities of the New Deal – particularly the N.R.A. – were given, on the whole, a hearty welcome by the rich man and were more than acceptable even to the rich man's press.

To be sure, the investor did not like the N.R.A. provisions which attempted to support wages as well as prices; but these provisions were largely evaded or ignored. It is significant, in view of the subsequent excitement about the President's Supreme Court plan and the investor's sudden solicitude for the Constitution, to recall the large measure of support given to the N.R.A. in the early months of Hugh Johnson's Blue Eagle regime. The N.R.A. was so completely, and almost so self-evidently, unconstitutional, that when it finally did reach the Supreme Court not a single Justice could cast his vote in its behalf. Yet the same forces which so vigorously rallied public opinion behind the Blue Eagle, not only condoned but applauded evasion and violation of constitutional legislation such as the Wagner Act. The big investor is commonly on the side of the law only because the law is commonly on the side of property rights. But whenever legislation is passed in the interest of human rights, the investor is stubbornly and viciously resistant to it.

The era of good feeling between the President and the capitalist did not survive the early stages of the New Deal. The split came chiefly over taxation. There were some 16,000,000 unemployed when Mr. Roosevelt took office. Not even the business man could deny the necessity for large relief appropriations. But as time went on, and as private industry failed to make progress in re-employing the idle, it became evident that the "relief problem," if not permanent, would at least require years to settle. The unemployed could be supported only by increasing taxes. And well before Mr. Roosevelt was up for reelection, the business man knew that many of these taxes would fall directly upon him.

The social security taxes and the undistributed profits tax were particularly irksome to the monopolistic corporations. That the taxes were by no means a crushing financial burden to these companies is shown by the fact that in 1937 the 960 Standard Statistics companies made 98% as much money (*after all tax payments*) as they had made in 1927. But the investor regarded them as a menace not to his property but to his profits; not to his invested capital but to his dividend return on it. Just as the principle of dividends before wages operated to create unemployment, so the principle of dividends before unemployment relief operated to destroy the initial harmony between the Old Guard and the New Deal. While the industrialist pretended to believe in relief, he was determined to hold it down to a minimum so that the relief taxes would do the least possible damage to the profits which it had again become possible for him to make.

Yet the industrialist did not come out with the open statement that since industry could not afford to pay relief taxes without jeopardizing dividend payments, then relief payments and relief taxes must be reduced. Indeed, industry's argument against taxes was, as much as possible, based on the concealment of its real motives. Year after year, for example, we have read and listened to countless head-shakings, finger-pointings, and solemn warnings about the unbalanced budget, the terrible deficits incurred by the Federal government, and the risk of a breakdown in government credit. Yet during these same years the same men who would not put their money into the securities of private industry have bought billions of dollars of Treasury bonds. There has never been a period in which the Treasury was able to offer bonds at such low interest and with so many takers. Granted they offer a tax-exempt revenue, nevertheless why has the investor any such confidence in a government which he claims to consider reckless, extravagant and radical, and so little confidence in private industry which he claims to consider cautious, thrifty, and wise? The answer is that he knows the Treasury can meet its obligations; he knows also that private industry, heavily overcapitalized during the boom period, cannot carry an increased capitalization without paying a smaller return on it. It is the credit of the Treasury that is good; the credit of private industry (for example, the railroad industry) that is bad. Yet the industrialist attempts to frighten uninformed persons through the use of arguments which he himself knows to be completely false.

An even more disgusting phase of the campaign against taxes for relief has been the constantly growing output of sneers and innuendos concerning the character of the jobless poor. In the early days of the New Deal the investor did not dare to refer to the jobless in uncomplimentary language. The people remembered too well that it was the rich man, not the poor man, who created unemployment. The market crash and the bank holiday were still too recent for industry to pretend that President Roosevelt had ruined the market or that radicals had closed the banks. But people have short memories and the newspapers still exert a tremendous influence on the public mind, not so much through their commonly fatuous editorials as through their faculty for editing their supposedly news columns. So hardly had the investor come crawling out of his safety deposit box before the attacks upon the unemployed began. For if that portion of the public which still had jobs could be persuaded that there were jobs open for all, or nearly all, right-thinking, clean-living Americans, the demand for relief might be dismissed as coming from an unworthy source.

Hence, for example, the sneers at "boon-doggling" — the attempt to discredit Administration-financed public work as an extravagant waste on useless projects. Here the argument was based on confusing the idea of production for use with the idea of production for profit. Suppose the New Deal *did* put up new post offices in places where the old post offices would have done very well. "Money wasting," cried the industrialist, his eyes full of tears. But these post offices were not built primarily to improve the national facilities for handling mail. They were built to put money into circulation. They circulated not only the money paid to relief workers but the money paid for materials and supplies. If the post offices had fallen to pieces the moment they were completed, the building job would still have achieved its major purpose.

The industrialist himself does not care whether the products of his industry serve any useful purpose. Generally they have a use value, otherwise they could not be sold. But this use value is not at all a part of the industrialist's purpose in producing goods. He will not produce anything, no matter how useful, if there is no profit in it. And

what, from the standpoint of producing useful
goods, is a more monstrous boon-doggle than the
business of building battleships and artillery and
military planes and bombs? If we are discussing
production for use, what is more idiotic than to
spend money making a useless shell to blow up a
useful house, to say nothing of the persons who
may be in the house when the shell hits it? Yet
the industrialist has no objections to wars. He
thrives on them. It is unfortunate that they involve casualties, but no better antidote to a depression has yet been found. Ask the German
capitalist, who has fallen back upon wars and
preparations for wars as his last chance for squeez-
ing profits out of poverty. Ask the Italian capitalist, who has already profited out of one official and
one unofficial military campaign.

The investor himself is in a particularly bad
position to talk about wasting money in non-
productive enterprises. In 1929 he put more than
two billion dollars of surplus capital into investment trusts organized for no productive purpose
whatsoever. They were formed to speculate in
the stock market, to buy stocks which had already
reached absurdly high prices in the hope that
they might reach even higher prices and be resold
to some even more reckless purchaser. Since the
investment trusts arrived in the very final stages

of the 1929 Bull Market—one of them, Blue
Ridge, a utility investment trust organized by
a Wall Street group, began selling its stock less
than three months before the big crash – they
were out on the very end of the limb when the
market broke. Investment trusts were a two-
billion-dollar boon-doggle, and the children of
Mammon, not even wise in their own generation,
lost nearly every dollar they had put into them.

That, presumably, was business. It certainly
exemplified the business judgment of the swollen
simpletons who in 1929 posed as the economic
messiahs of the United States. But to spend money
on projects which, if not essential to society, were
certainly not harmful to it was regarded as a terrible waste and an appalling extravagance. The
fact that relief money supported millions of men
and women whom industry could not or would not
support was ignored. Even the purchasing power
created by the money paid relief workers was entirely overlooked, although every penny of that
money went instantly into circulation via the nearest store that sold things to eat or things to wear.
The only *sincere* objection that business had to the
money spent on relief was that a part – by
no means all – of the relief funds came from business through taxation.

From sneers at boon-doggling the rich man

passed into more contemptible sneers at the relief workers themselves. Even the newspapers had to show a certain measure of caution in their published statements concerning relief applicants. But they went as far as they dared and the word-of-mouth campaign went a great deal further. The propaganda is too familiar to need repetition. Jokes about how long it took relief workers to do a job. Stupid and vicious generalizations that the unemployed would not work "no matter what you paid them". Smart remarks about people who "made a career" of the WPA. A whole campaign of malicious falsehood designed to convey the impression that the unemployed were vagrants and vagabonds, that people who really tried to get work could always get it, that the worker and not the employer was responsible for unemployment.

It is a matter of astonishment that this attempt to make villains out of victims actually seems to have made some impression upon the public, even upon the lower middle class public that is hanging on the brink of unemployment relief itself. The housewife, whose white-collar husband is wondering when it will be his turn to be fired, complains that you cannot possibly get servants nowadays because the worthless creatures would rather loaf on relief money. What she should say is that she cannot get servants for even less than the semi-starvation wages offered to the relief worker.* It would undoubtedly suit the interests of the sweatshop operator, whether he runs a little sweat shop in Manhattan or an enormous sweat shop in North Carolina, to eliminate relief work so that the unemployed could be hired en masse for $5 or $6 a week. It remains difficult to see why such a consideration should have any influence except upon the anti-social individuals who would profit by it.

No one who looks at the unemployment situation with the least pretence to reason and impartiality will maintain that the unemployed are jobless because they are unable or unwilling to work. There are today somewhere around 12,-000,000 unemployed in this country — over one-fifth of the total number of persons who would have jobs if conditions of full employment existed. Derogatory generalizations about such a large group are obviously senseless. As has been said, you cannot libel a nation, and even one-fifth of a nation is still too large for slander. Between October 1, 1937, and May 1, 1938, over 4,000,000 workers lost their jobs. Did these men become lazy and shiftless overnight? In May, 1938 (according to the U. S. Department of Labor

* Average WPA payment in August, 1938, was $58 a month.

figures), 300,000 more workers were fired. Did these men suddenly decide that they would throw down their tools and live in luxurious idleness at the public's expense? It should not be necessary to ask these questions which obviously supply their own answers.

The misrepresentations of the industrialist are particularly significant because they show the extent to which he relies upon false issues. The whole campaign of the reactionary is based either on an inability to reason or a desire to deceive.

Consider the difference between the real and the pretended objections to the President's plan for enlarging the Supreme Court. The real objections were obvious enough. Mr. Landon had just been defeated even more decisively than Mr. Hoover. The popular endorsement of the New Deal was so whole-hearted that even those members of Congress who were Democrats in name only were ready to go along with the President. There was no telling what Mr. Roosevelt, reinforced by his second great victory, might do. But there was never any uncertainty about the attitude of the Supreme Court. In Mr. Roosevelt's first term, many vital Administration measures had been blocked by the conservative Justices. Many other essential pieces of legislation were still to come before the high court. Whatever future plans the New

Dealers might have would eventually have to pass its scrutiny.

As neither House nor Senate could afford to ignore the popular mandate which the New Deal had just received, the last refuge of the reactionary was his fellow reactionaries on the Supreme Court bench. Appointed to office for life, totally independent of public opinion, the "conservative" majority of the Supreme Court could still be relied upon to ignore what the many wanted and to protect what the few possessed. No comprehensive program of New Deal legislation could be passed over the opposition of the United States Supreme Court as it was constituted in February, 1937. The "nine old men" were the keepers of the keys, the watch-dogs of the dividends. When the President proposed to enlarge the court, he was attacking the last stronghold of the reactionary. He was attempting to remove the one barrier to progress on which the enemies of progress most confidently relied.

But what was the burden of the reactionary opposition to the Court plan? Chiefly that it represented dictatorship, or that it took such a long step toward dictatorship that the liberties of the people were imperiled. This argument was, of course, entirely false. There are two essential characteristics which any measure leading toward dictatorship must possess. In the first place, it must contain an element of coercion. In the second place, it must contain an element of illegality. There was nothing coercive in Mr. Roosevelt's proposal. The fact that it was defeated is sufficient evidence of that. Nor was it in any sense illegal. The Constitution does not say how many Supreme Court Justices there should be; the number has been increased in the past and may be increased again in the future. Had the President attempted to appoint new Justices without having the appointments confirmed by the Senate, the situation would have been very different. But there was nothing dictatorial in the President's orderly, legitimate, and extremely constructive proposal as it was actually presented, whatever criticisms might have been made of its precise form.

In 1911, the liberals of England proposed to alter an ancient British institution even more radically than the President proposed to change the U. S. Supreme Court. At that time, measures passed by the House of Commons had also to be passed by the House of Lords before they became a part of British law. The House of Lords therefore had what amounted to a veto power over the Commons. Like the Supreme Court, the House of Lords was a group of non-elected dignitaries with a lifetime tenure of office and was completely independent of the public's will. It had been demonstrating this independence in 1909 by refusing to accept an appropriation bill ("The People's Budget") proposed by the British Liberal Government and passed by the Liberal-controlled Commons. The Liberal program called for a large increase in the taxes of the very rich, to be spent largely in attempting to improve the condition of the poor. British Tories saw no more merit in these proposals than American Tories see in relief taxation today. And the House of Lords, by refusing to accept this money-raising measure embodying taxes obnoxious to the land-holding class which it largely represented, had been blocking the Liberal program, just as Supreme Court decisions were blocking the progress of the New Deal.

But one of the prerogatives of the British Crown is the right to create new peers. It was possible for the King to make a Lord out of anybody. This prerogative had frequently been exercised — at the instance of various ministries — in behalf of low-blooded but high-incomed persons who had contributed largely to the campaign funds of whichever British party happened to be in power. Indeed, the British peerage was sometimes referred to as the "beerage," the reference being to the large number of brewers who had purchased titles to which they had not been born.

The 1909 crisis had been solved by the Liberal Government's introduction of an even more radical measure: the framing of a bill which nullified the power of the House of Lords by providing that any measure passed by three sessions of Commons would become a law even without the consent of the Lords. The Lords passed the appropriation bill. But against the new bill (called the Parliament Bill), they were prepared to fight to the finish.

It was then—after twice going to the people for support on the issue — that the Liberal Prime Minister, Mr. Asquith, announced that King George was ready to bring his Lord-creating privilege into action. Mr. Asquith told the leaders of the House of Lords that unless they accepted the Parliament Bill on its second reading, the King would create enough new peers, of Liberal leanings, to bring about a Liberal majority in the House of Lords itself. Terrified at this possibility — it meant enlarging the House to the extent of 400 or 500 new peers — the Lords gave in and the bill passed. The Tories, it is true, also became semi-hysterical about precedents and "puppet peers" but the Liberals' bill went through and the British people soon had other and even more important matters to occupy their minds.

In this country, however, the Court Bill was

defeated, although it passed the House and would probably have passed the Senate except through almost incredibly bad management on the Senate floor. It was defeated on the wholly irrelevant issue of dictatorship, an issue easy to raise today because of the apparent weakness of world democracy. Indeed, the "dictatorship" propaganda was again successfully unlimbered to defeat the President's plan for reorganizing the various departments of the Federal Government – a totally innocuous measure embodying no more sweeping changes than Mr. Coolidge and Mr. Hoover had previously recommended. It is unquestionably true that the Supreme Court has by this time become relatively liberalized, but the moral effect of the reactionaries victory remains undiminished. The Court Plan may yet go down in history as the Gettysburg of the New Deal.

I should like to give one further instance of reactionary hypocrisy, as it represents a technique which, unfortunately, still flourishes. In the spring of 1937, when both Republicans and Democrats wished themselves into believing that the depression was over, the revival in business activity led to a corresponding revival in the effort to organize labor. The opposition of the employers of labor to the organizing of their employes resulted in a series of strikes. The most notorious of these struggles against organized labor was the refusal of the so-called "independent" steel companies (Republic, Inland, Youngstown, and Bethlehem) to recognize the C.I.O. as bargaining agent. Under the Wagner Act, as passed by Congress and confirmed by the Supreme Court, the employer was obligated to deal with any organization chosen by his employes. Tom Girdler, president of Republic Steel, took the position that he would not contract with the C.I.O. because the C.I.O. was not the kind of organization that *he* felt like dealing with. There is nothing in the Wagner Act that gives employers any right to pass upon the qualifications of the union their workers form. Obviously such power would result in the recognition of no union except possibly some innocuous "company union" controlled by the bosses and not by the men. Mr. Girdler might just as well have refused to honor workmen's compensation acts on the ground that he did not consider some worker, injured in line of duty, a person fit to be compensated. Again and again Mr. Girdler repeated that the C.I.O. did not deserve to be negotiated with, and every time that he made this statement* he was discussing a point which had nothing to do with the situation in which he found himself.

* Mr. Girdler spoke in these terms: "The real issues have to do with the nature and character of the parties involved. . . . Must Republic and its men submit to the Communistic dictates and terrorism of the C.I.O.?"

Yet when, in the face of this arbitrary and unjustifiable attitude, the steel workers called their strike, all but a handful of the newspapers did their best to reinforce Mr. Girdler's position. When public and private police attacked strikers' meetings and broke up picket lines, the occasions were referred to as "riots" and the strikers were transformed into "mobs." When small-town politicians, business men, professional patriots, and other leaders of the more misguided section of public opinion formed "law-and-order" leagues nothing was said about the fact that the steel owners were acting in defiance of the law of the United States and the order of the Supreme Court. Those workers who were so deluded, so cowed, or so needy as to remain at their jobs were called "loyal" workers, although precisely what they were supposed to be "loyal" to was never defined. The reactionary became almost sentimental in his defence of the "loyal worker" and the loyal worker's "right to work," although six months later these same workers were being laid off by the thousands and their "right to work" was not talked about any more.

The fact that the C.I.O., as a national union, necessarily has national officers not immediately identified with any of its local branches, and that these officers are necessarily prominent in the conduct of a strike, was the basis for denunciation of "outside interference." The outside union had outside organizers. The outside organizers were commonly described as outside agitators. But of course the outside agitator might be an alien agitator. And, even more self-evidently, the alien agitator was almost certainly a Communist. The terminus of this train of thought was the sweeping generalization that the peace and quiet of Ohio, Pennsylvania, and Illinois had been invaded by a gang of Reds against whom, as a matter of self-protection, it was necessary to call out the police and the militia.

The outcome of this campaign of distortion and misrepresentation came on Memorial Day, 1937, when striking Republic Steel workers in Chicago, peacefully demonstrating in the vicinity of Republic's Chicago plant, were brutally and inexcusably attacked by the Chicago police, who killed ten strikers and injured a hundred others. All of the ten dead were shot to death. There was no evidence that the strikers were armed. There were many women among them. They were engaged in holding a demonstration, not in conducting an onslaught upon either Republic's property or Republic's men. There was no battle — the police did not report a singly fatality among their ranks. The reactionary, I suppose, remembers Chicago's Memorial Day (when he is forced to remember it at all) as a "riot." The workers remember it as a massacre.

The men killed that day were not enemies of society. They were not committing any crime. They were engaged in asserting the right of labor to organize in its own way and under its own leaders, a right recently and expressly granted to them by the Government of the United States. But the propaganda of the industrialist and of his publishing and political camp-followers had so completely obscured that right and so viciously misrepresented the position of these men that it became possible for the Chicago police to pass and execute a death-penalty upon them. And the same newspapers which had so largely contributed to the public's ignorance and misinformation concerning the Little Steel strike published such prejudiced and misleading accounts of the Chicago "riot" that it was quite possible to conclude from them that the strikers were attempting to take Republic's plant to pieces brick by brick or that the police had fired upon them only as a last resort and purely in self-defense.

It is, perhaps, hardly necessary to add that the real reason for the Little Steel companies' refusal to deal with the C.I.O. was a purely financial one. The editorial apologists for Mr. Girdler and his fellow C.I.O.-haters themselves gave away the show when they argued that recognition of the C.I.O. was only the first step toward the closed shop and the check-off. Here again an issue entirely irrelevant was being raised, for the C.I.O. strike embraced nothing but union recognition. It is true that the steel companies were afraid that union recognition would lead to an argument about higher wages, and were also afraid that an openly recognized union which the workers could not be intimidated from joining would attract so many members that no "loyal" workers would remain. But those were bridges which the steel companies were bound, both in law and in ethics, to cross only when they came to them. To balk at recognition itself was merely to advertise the fact that Republic, Youngstown, Inland, and Bethlehem suspected they were paying to unorganized labor wages for which organized labor would never stand. The basis of the anti-union stand taken by the independent steel companies was the fear that union recognition would lead to increased wage costs and possibly to reduced dividends. In a larger sense it represented the industrialist's hostility to any organization which would interfere with his control of costs by interfering with his control of wages. But this strictly financial issue was hidden under all manner of excuses, evasions, distortions, and downright lies.

It would be easy to cite a great many more examples of the false fronts behind which the industrialist hides. But we have already seen that his basic disguise is the concealment of an economic issue behind an ethical issue — an appeal to right and wrong designed to cover his interest in dollars and cents. Under Mr. Hoover, the industrialist was allowed to take a strictly deflationary course; wages were cut, production was cut, and even price structures were sometimes abandoned in the hope that the depression, given a free hand, would eventually run its course. Unfortunately, purchasing power shrank even more rapidly than prices and production, and the nation went down and down until it was on the brink, economically, of going down and out. Industry was left in the awkward position of having to be bailed out by a man whom it then regarded with suspicion and whom it now regards with hate. Nor could the old handouts about prosperity-for-the-boss-being-prosperity-for-everyone be any longer relied upon to answer every criticism of the economic system. Industry's traditional story had been found to contain so many wrong answers that even the dullest pupil had begun to realize that teacher really did not have the least suspicion of what everything was all about.

So, driven from its economic basis, industry

shifted to a psychological basis. It is remarkable how much of the propaganda of the reactionary during the past five years has been an appeal to fear. Probably the appeal has been the more effective because it has been advanced during a period in which a majority of the population has been so constantly dominated by the fear of losing the job. At any rate, the technique of the reactionary has been largely a scare technique.

Thus relief expenditures should be cut because they unbalanced the budget and an unbalanced budget would lead to runaway inflation or national bankruptcy or something of the same dreadful sort. Social security taxes were little better than a swindle because the Administration would be holding the people's money until they reached the age of 65, and God knows if the Administration would have any left then. The unemployed were not only no-goods, bums, and loafers, but they were all shot through with communism and what was the use of coddling a bunch of discontented vagrants who might bring the whole country down into the gutters from which they sprang? New Deal legislation, particularly the Supreme Court plan, was not only half-baked socialism but was also designed to make a dictator out of Franklin D. Roosevelt. The Congressman who supported the New Deal was merely a "rubber stamp" for Führer Franklin.

It must be admitted that the strategy of the reactionary was good strategy, although what his advertising agencies would call the "fear appeal" perhaps came naturally to him because he was badly scared himself. However, the public as a whole was even more badly frightened and with better reason, for although there was not much danger of the rich man losing his wealth there was constant danger that the poor man would lose even the little that he had.

There have been occasions on which the fear psychology of the industrialist has developed into very definite threats. In Akron, Ohio, the tire manufacturers (Goodyear, Firestone, Goodrich) have repeatedly threatened to move out of town unless "labor conditions" are made more to their liking. Here is an attempt to coerce not only the rubber workers of Akron but the entire city. It shows how completely the point of view of the industrialist has altered. Ten years ago he was promising universal prosperity provided he were allowed unlimited profits. Now he threatens a community with economic destruction unless he is given a free hand with labor. In Philadelphia, a strike at the Philco Radio & Television Corp. produced much the same situation, with Philco threatening to leave Philadelphia unless police or military protection was provided for the re-opening of the plant.

It is true that threats like these are largely bluffs. The tire makers, for instance, have hundreds of millions of dollars invested in Akron plant and property. No corporation manager could justify to his stockholders the cost of abandoning an existing plant, let alone the cost of duplicating it elsewhere. Yet the bluff has its effect on business men, merchants and the community in general. Knowing that only the most intolerable conditions could justify an exodus, citizens conclude that the intolerable conditions must exist because the exodus is threatened. They should realize the great difference between talking about leaving town and actually going. They should also realize that such talk is an attempt by the corporations to intimidate the community.

In a larger sense, however, the corporations can and do reduce the benefits of social legislation by means of their antisocial response to it. A wage-and-hour bill which provides for a 40-hour week at a minimum of 40 cents an hour is socially desirable and will provide more wages for more workers. But the net gain will not be as great as the apparent gain, because employers who consider $16 a week a maximum rather than a minimum wage will keep their payrolls down by firing some of the men who work for them. The proposed railroad pay-cut was another example of the same condition. Railroad wages averaged between 60 cents and 70 cents an hour. Many railroad workers were unemployed, or, as the railroads call it, "on furlough." When the railroad unions refused to accept the cut, the roads furloughed as many more men as possible. There is fortunately an irreducible minimum of employes beneath which the roads cannot well operate. Manufacturing, also, has become so highly mechanized that the further substitution of machines for men is becoming more difficult. Yet the corporation manager will continue, to the best of his ability, to resist attempts to increase or to maintain his payroll by exercising his power to reduce the number of men on it.

There was a time when the few made promises to the many. Ten years ago the few were boasting about the American standard of living, the two-car garage, the chicken in every pot. At that time, however, they were expanding. They were making new profit records every year. Now they are contracting. Profits are more difficult to gather, dividends more difficult to pay. The industrialist considers it no longer possible to be social-minded and shareholder-minded as well. He used to make promises to the public. Today he is making threats.

Chapter XI

DEPRESSION IS OUR NORMAL STATE

As I have already said, I see no reason why the 1940's should be any better than the 1930's. There is, indeed, every reason to believe that they may be considerably worse. Our population increases at the rate of almost a million a year. Our schools and colleges graduate close to 2,000,000 job-hunting boys and girls every June. Even allowing for the disappearance of workers through (industrial) old age and death, our net increase in job-hunters is more than 700,000 per annum. It is becoming constantly more difficult for the man over forty to get a job or even (unless he has an executive position) to keep one. By 1950 the population of working age will be at least 7,000,000 greater than it is today.

Nor does it follow that a natural increase in population is accompanied by a corresponding natural increase in jobs. The manufacturing industry, for example, employed more workers in 1918 than it has in any subsequent year. The great increase in manufacturing output during the 1920's was accomplished with very little increase in manufacturing jobs, the additional output coming from the use of more machinery, not from the use of more men. Post-1929 output has of course never approached 1929 totals, and a marked increase in mechanization has made manual labor even more superfluous than it was when times were good.

Furthermore, the Thirties probably saw only a small increase in non-manufacturing jobs – in those jobs which, when discussing the automobile business, I referred to as *derivative* jobs created by manufacturing although not on the manufacturer's payroll. I doubt whether the total number of automobiles in use will show much sustained increase during the next ten years. There will not be much demand for more filling stations, more truck drivers, more taxi men, more drillers of oil or refiners of gasoline. The big apartment houses that support doormen and "superintendents" and elevator operators are now rarely being built; even more unusual is the appearance of the skyscraper with its many jobs for those who service it.

To be sure, the next decade will no doubt produce *some* increase in employment, since the wants of those who are to be born in the next ten years cannot go entirely unfilled. But there is almost certain to be a marked discrepancy between population growth and occupational opportunity. This discrepancy may express itself in terms of increased unemployment. It is perhaps more likely to express itself in lower wages and a lower standard of living all around. It is not an accident that the National Labor Relations Board is by all odds the most unpopular of the New Deal agencies — that is, the most unpopular from the employer's point of view. For the NLRB is the greatest single obstacle to the open-shop, low-paid labor which is the industrialist's chief answer to the problems of the day.

Yet in spite of the fact that underlying economic conditions indicate a period of depression for many years to come, nearly everyone persists in regarding prosperity as our normal state. Sometimes I think that until we get a working generation which does not remember 1929, we shall be forever hypnotized by the recollection of that gaudy period. Certainly the word "recovery" appears to have an unbreakable grip upon our present consciousness. Let businesses indices improve a little, let the Market pursue an upward course for more than two consecutive weeks, let there be even the slightest reduction in the ranks of the unemployed — and everyone is speculating as to whether we are really on our way back to 1929. As I have already said, back to 1929 is the most certain method of getting also back to 1932, but most of us would be happy to accept the boom and hopeful of escaping the crash.

So strong is the conviction that business is naturally good and that only some malign influence can make it bad, that the New Deal's strongest talking point today is the depth which the Depression reached under Mr. Hoover's presidency. But, by the same reasoning, the Republican's most effective argument is found in the fact that seven years of the New Deal have not made the country prosperous. Not long ago I heard Representative Martin, the Republican leader in the House, exhort all working people to vote the Republican ticket in order to get off the WPA and get themselves a "real job." There is a good deal of truth in the part about getting off the WPA. The part about getting the "real job," however, contains a pronounced element of fantasy.

It is true, nevertheless, that the New Deal has had almost two full Administrations in which to do its work, and that the state of the nation is still precarious. For this unfortunate circumstance the New Deal is not responsible. If it were not for the New Dealers, conditions would probably be very much worse than they are. But the New Dealers *are* responsible for the political capital which their opponents are making out of the continuance of

bad times. For they themselves have been constantly chasing the rainbow of recovery. They
themselves have expected each new pump-priming
effort to be the last. At the time of the 1936–1937
recovery – such as it was – Mr. Roosevelt publicly proclaimed that the New Dealers had "planned it that way," that conditions were better
because they had been made better by the policies
and the program of the New Deal. It was inevitable
that when, in the fall of 1937, the shaky structure
of recovery collapsed, the Republicans wanted to
know if the President had again "planned it that
way," and if the general catastrophe was another
fruit of the New Deal tree.

Doubtless no administration can avoid responsibility for whatever happens while it is in office.
Poor Mr. Hoover certainly did not bring about the
Depression; his major error lay in remaining so
long unaware of it. But during the 1934–1936 recovery period (recovery, at least, from the total
collapse of 1933) the Democrats not only accepted
but claimed responsibility for everything that took
place. And now they are being haunted by 1937
as the Republicans were haunted by 1932. Yet it
is beyond the power of any administration, Demo-
crat or Republican, to bring about an alteration of
fundamental economic trends. For some 150 years
in this country we have kept the government out

of business, although we have not always kept business out of the government. And today, in any essential particular, no administration can be more to business than an outsider looking in.

The New Deal's major effort to promote recovery has been through its work-relief and farm-relief programs. The only sound criticism that can be made of the expenditures involved in these programs is that the expenditures have not been large enough. But, in a broader sense, they represent an alleviation but not a cure. When a man has a broken leg, you can ease his suffering by giving him a narcotic. But you do not thereby do anything to make the leg better.

The New Deal theory, to be sure, has not been that relief expenditures should in themselves bring about a recovery. The Administration's idea has been that these payments would be sufficient to renew business activity which, once going again, would pick up speed on its own initiative. But to ask of "pump priming" that it should be even a prelude to recovery is to ask too much of it.

If 12,000,000 "employables" now not at work in private industry were employed at an average wage of $20 a week, their annual pay would come to twenty four billion dollars. (If you wish to take the unduly low estimate of 10,000,000 unemployed, the annual wage would be twenty billion dollars.) Inasmuch as our productive capacity is geared to conditions of full employment, we may say that there is a twenty four billion dollar gap between what our producers can produce and what our consumers could consume if they had the money to buy it with. It is true that our producing plant can do very nicely when it is running at 80% or even 75% of its capacity. But even this elasticity is far from sufficient to take up the slack that unemployment has caused.

Meanwhile, during the entire ten years of the Depression, relief payments have not come to anything in the neighborhood of twenty four billion dollars or of twenty billion dollars either. They have not averaged as much as two billion a year. If you give $2 to a man who needs $24, you may enable him to provide himself with a cup of coffee and a doughnut, but he is not going to be much in the market for steaks, shoes and houses. We cannot reasonably expect pump-priming even to pave the way for recovery unless we practice pump-priming at four or five times its recent rate. I do not say that it is possible for the government to distribute relief money on an eight or ten billion dollar a year basis. (I do say that the Government's credit, which the conservative professes to find in such danger, could stand a much greater strain than has thus far been imposed upon it.) But it should be evident that the shrinkage of consumer buying power, through unemployment, has gone far beyond the compensating effect of relief expenditures.

Furthermore, a great many persons who are rated as employed, because they do *some* work every week, should better be considered as part-time employed because they work *so few hours* each week. A man who works 40 hours a week for 70 cents an hour, has a $28 a week job. The same man, working 20 hours a week for 70 cents an hour, still has a job. But it is not a $28 a week job. It is a $14 a week job. One hundred such men represent no more purchasing power than fifty men on the 40 hour basis. Yet one hundred men at 20 hours a week are counted as just as much "employment" as one hundred men at the longer week.

The importance of this point is illustrated by a recent report of the United States Steel Corpora-· tion. During the first half of 1938, U. S. Steel had an average employment of 206,357 men. Its output for these six months was approximately 3,000,000 tons of steel. Its payroll was about $135,000,000.

During the first six months of 1939, U. S. Steel's output reflected improved business conditions and rose to 4,400,000 tons. This output was an increase of 45% over the output for the first half of 1938.

But average employment for the first six months of 1939 was 206,113 men. There was no increase over employment for the first half of 1938 — in fact, the current year showed a decline of 244 men.

To be sure, the payroll was considerably increased. It rose to $165,000,000 — an increase of about 20%. In other words, the same number of men worked about 20% more man-hours. Notice, however, that a 45% increase in production was recorded with a 20% increase in pay. Here is a tribute to the labor-saving machinery which U. S. Steel (and industry in general) has installed during the depression years. But it is another indication of how long unemployment (and therefore the Depression) will last.

A good many morals could be drawn from the figures just cited. At the moment, however, I am most interested in pointing out that the Steel Corporation turned out almost three tons of steel in the first half of 1939 to every two tons of steel turned out in the first half of 1938, without hiring any more men. The improvement in production was very substantial. But it was secured without any lessening in the number of unemployed steel workers. (Even at the improved output figure, the Steel Corporation was only running at about 49% of capacity, so there was still plenty of room for more steel without a corresponding number of new workers.)

U. S. Steel made a profit ($1,970,311) for the first half of 1939. It had lost $6,302,577 during the first half of 1938. A two-million dollar profit in six months is not much for U. S. Steel. Still, the existence of any profit showed that the Steel Corporation had reached and passed its break-even point. In comparison with 1938, at least, 1939 was a prosperous period. Yet this prosperity brought no new employment.

So the problem is: *How much* will the business tempo have to accelerate before any considerable reduction in the number of unemployed can be made? I do not know the answer to this question. But I am certain that relief expenditures are not sufficient to bring about the necessary speeding-up.

Relief-money should not be regarded as a means of restoring prosperity. It is no more than an inadequate means of somewhat reducing the hunger of those who would otherwise starve.

It is true that relief expenditures are not the only item in the New Deal program. Yet other New Deal measures, although many of them are admirable in intent, must be considered under the heading of reform rather than under the heading of recovery. Thus the Social Security Act, whatever may be its long term benefits, is for the time being a hindrance to recovery because of the money which it takes out of circulation. The Tennessee Valley Authority, although it may reduce the cost of electricity in its immediate neighborhood, would be significant only as a forerunner of Federal electricity on a national scale. The Securities and Exchange Commission has been more successful than any other New Deal agency in accomplishing what it was organized to do. But the abuses which prompted the creation of the SEC are essentially abuses associated with a Bull Market and the SEC had no noticeable influence either on the speculative enthusiasm of late 1936 or the speculative catastrophe in late 1937. The undistributed profits tax was important because it showed a faint recognition of the fact that all corporations are not alike, but Congress first emasculated it and then wiped it out. I do not think that any of the New Deal reforms actually interfere with recovery, but neither do they contribute to it.

And the New Deal does suffer a good deal from its apparent conviction that a fundamental evil can be corrected by passing a law concerning one of its superficial aspects. This weakness results largely from the fact that the personnel of the New Deal is so largely made up of lawyers who, naturally enough, are fond of framing laws. It is also unfortunate that most of the lawyers would have difficulty in distinguishing between a fixed asset and a floating kidney. Many of their ideas would have been more appropriate in the time of the first Roosevelt than they are in the time of the second. There are many horse-and-buggy concepts in which the animal and the vehicle are standing on the liberal side of the fence.

A characteristic example of reform thinking is seen in the movement toward "unscrambling" the "oversized" corporations and restoring competition by recreating smaller corporate units. Advocates of this procedure would take the major divisions of the big companies, or the major original components of merged companies, and set them up as separate and allegedly competitive concerns. Thus General Motors would be carved up into a Cadillac Co., a Buick Co., a Chevrolet Co., a Fisher Body Co., a Frigidaire Co., and so on. The Aluminum Co. would be broken up into at least two new companies – one Aluminum Co. to produce the metal and another to fabricate it. And a company such as National Steel might be disassembled into the Weirton Steel Co., the Great Lakes Steel Co. and the Hanna Ore Co. – these being the three companies which were merged into National Steel in 1929. The general application of such a technique would result in the creation of perhaps 10,000 or 20,000 large companies out of the 1,000 large companies which now dominate our industrial life.

There are many legal and financial obstacles in the way of separating large companies into their component parts. It would, for instance, be difficult to divide the cash and securities of General Motors among its various operating units. And the stockholders of large companies, arguing that the profits of the companies are dependent upon their size, might claim that the return on their investment was being jeopardized and their property rights being taken away. But even if the big companies could be divided, it does not at all follow that competition would be restored by dividing them.

For the ownership of the new companies would remain exactly the same as the ownership of the old company. If one man, or a group of men, owned 10% of the stock of a merged company, he would have to be given 10% of the stock in each of its unmerged fragments. Otherwise the process of unmerging would amount to downright confiscation. And corporate units which have no corporate connection are not truly independent as long as they have a common ownership. The stockholders of the Cadillac Co., the Buick Co., the Chevrolet Co. and of other companies that might be manufactured out of the General Motors company would have every reason to see that the "new" corporations continued to do exactly what the old divisions of General Motors had been doing. Into no matter how many companies the Aluminum Co. might be divided, the Mellon interests would still have large holdings in all the pieces, and would take care that the new companies avoided stepping on each other's toes. If the National Steel Co. were disassembled into Weirton Steel, Great Lakes Steel and Hanna Ore, Ernest Weir (of Weirton), George Fink (of Great Lakes) and the Hanna family would have large interest in the three new corporations. There is no reason to believe that Mr. Weir would fight with Mr. Fink, or that the Hanna family would fight with either of the other two.

We have already seen that large companies in which there is no community of ownership get along with a minimum of competition. How then can we anticipate competition from new companies with the same stockholders? It makes little difference into how many sections you carve an existing company if the proprietors of the new companies are also the proprietors of the old concern. You might as well forbid the eight arms of an octopus to act in concert, while not disturbing the round part in the middle that contains the nerve centers of the creature. Thus any program of unscrambling the big companies is based on a failure to recognize the nature of the issues involved.

A similar lack of realism is shown in most of the other suggestions which are from time to time advanced as the solution of our problems. The idea of regulating all big businesses as the railroads and power companies are now regulated may be appealing at first sight. But any form of regulation, to have any real force, would inevitably involve the government in wide-spread price-fixing covering thousands of products manufactured by hundreds of com₊anies. An Interstate Commerce Commission, or its equivalent, attempting to fix the prices of radios, tin cans, adding machines, steam shovels, bicarbonate of soda, Diesel engines, and scrap iron — to say nothing of the prices of butter and eggs — could result only in dictatorship or in chaos. The N.R.A. — a short lived experiment in fixing *minimum* prices — was perhaps justifiable as an emergency measure, but a permanent N.R.A. (in addition to being unconstitutional) would merely legalize the technique of price structures on which monopolistic industries are founded.

Furthermore, prices are only one end of a seesaw of which wages are the other. Low prices mean nothing if wages experience a corresponding decline. But if regulation leads to price control and price control leads to wage control, then we might as well make up our minds to turn business altogether over to the government. Whether government ownership and operation of industry would be a good thing is a point which I can hardly here debate.* But I very much doubt whether the persons who advocate greater "regulation" of industry appreciate the implications of their program.

A somewhat recent example of the reforming instinct is seen in the movement for "paid" or for "public" directors. It is true that a majority of corporate directors do not take their directing jobs with much seriousness. It is also true that, except in times of unusual crisis, the Board of Directors tends to ratify, with little question, the decisions of the management. On the other hand, many of the largest corporations have on their Boards one or more banker-directors who represent the large stockholders and speak with authority when vital decisions are to be made. But these men are not concerned with the interests of the small stockholder or with the interests of the public as a whole. And the usual director gives his job little time and less thought.

It has therefore been suggested that a new industrial job — the job of paid director — be

---

* It is commonly advocated by those who say that "the people" should own everything. But the people and the government are not at all the same thing. The closest approach that a modern State can make toward control by the people is control by a party. And that is not a system which recommends itself to many American minds.

created. The paid director is visualized as a man who spends all his time directing. He may work for only one corporation; he would hardly work for more than two or three. He would be adequately compensated for the time and energy consumed by his directing duties and he would in return be expected to make himself thoroughly familiar with the corporation's affairs. Then when the management, through greed, stupidity or downright dishonesty, proposed some action contrary to the best interests of the corporation, the paid director would put his finger in the dyke and his spoke in the wheel.

Something of this sort might work out with respect to small companies doing business on a small scale. But the notion approaches the ridiculous when applied to companies such as International Harvester or Allied Chemical & Dye or any other corporation of major size. No man who is in any sense outside the management of companies such as these can possibly make himself familiar with their activities. Any man of such outstanding ability, such remarkable judgment as to be competent for such a job would already have a good deal less anomalous position with a corporation or a banking house. Possibly a local flour mill might get some retired banker to advise it on when to put up an addition to its plant, but no large scale operation could possibly be subjected to the advice, let alone the control, of any outside man. Besides, if the "paid director" stayed long enough and worked hard enough to become a factor in the affairs of the concern, he would simply be one more insider, up to his ears in corporate politics and management cliques.

The reformer tends to be a romanticist. He looks at problems too much in terms of individuals and too little in terms of the issues involved. When he becomes frightened of "the man on horse-back," he thinks that the danger may be avoided by putting in another man to prevent the first man from getting on the horse. I cannot repeat too often that the troubles of our times are not caused by individual stupidity or individual dis-honesty. The Van Sweringens may have lost a lot of "other people's money," but they certainly did nothing more culpable than attempting to run a shoestring into an empire, a practice in the best tradition of American trade. The banking houses which distributed securities of South American governments may have realized that these issues were hardly on a par with the obligations of the U. S. Treasury. On the other hand, I doubt whether any number of paid directors could have persuaded these distributors to have included in their prospectuses a Short History of Latin American Defaults. Much as we may all believe that honesty is the best policy, there is no association between an improvement in the business conscience and an improvement in the business trend.

I have perhaps discussed reforms and experiments in detail out of proportion to their importance. It is also true that many reforming ideas (such as the paid directors) are in no sense a part of the New Deal program. But I think that what are commonly called "liberal" ideas are worth some consideration if only for the sake of suggesting that the liberal-minded person is often so far from being contemporary-minded and approaches the present situation with so little knowledge of its nature and complexity that he brings discredit upon any form of thinking which is not entirely satisfied with the status quo.

Yet should the public, in protest against continued hard times and in disappointment over the failure of the New Deal to resurrect the dead Twenties, turn to the conservative formula for recovery it will only invite a more profound disappointment and a more lasting disillusionment. The Republican approach to recovery can only be a deflationary approach. A Republican administration would necessarily reduce taxes, greatly decrease the number of persons on relief rôles, and either amend the Wagner Act in such a manner as virtually to repeal it or accomplish the same result by "packing" the National Labor Relations Board with corporation-minded administrators. I do not say that a Republican Administration would do these things with any sinister notion of depriving the people of its liberty or of casting the shadow of Fascism across our fair land. These measures represent the very minimum that any Administration elected on a recovery-through-business platform could possibly perform. They would be only mild expressions of a philosophy which is held by a great many otherwise intelligent men, and would be endorsed by the Owen Youngs and the Alfred Sloans as much as by the Tom Girdlers and the Ernest Weirs.

I have heard it argued that even a Republican administration would not greatly curtail relief because of the political unpopularity of such a measure. Yet only recently a Congress with a majority of titular Democrats passed a relief bill which will take several hundred thousand men and women off the WPA. An admittedly conservative Congress would go much farther in the same direction, probably under the pretense of handing the relief problem back to the States. The State Legislatures would then proceed to allow relief recipients very much less relief money than the amount the Federal government is now paying them but the national Administration would have successfully passed the responsibility for the welfare of the jobless into other hands.

Meanwhile, the industrialist would be given a free hand in a drive toward low wages and no unions. Here again the national government would not have to incur any direct responsibility. There would be strikes. There would be "riots." There would be bloodshed. But these unfortunate incidents could readily be handled by private and public police, vigilantes or, in cases of extreme emergency, the militia. Meanwhile some deserving Republican would be establishing himself as the greatest Secretary of the Treasury since, let us say, Andrew Mellon.

But what of the theory that a revival of business confidence would bring about a revival of prosperity? In the first place, this theory rests upon the false premise that capital is hiding away in the banks because it is afraid that the present Administration may enact some drastic measure against the sanctity of private property. If, at the moment, any capitalist still retains any such concept of the New Deal, he should call in a psychiatrist and see what can be done about his persecution complex.

Capital is not lying low because it is frightened about the New Deal. It is lying low because it knows that the money already invested in our industrial plant has produced so much excess capacity that it is difficult to find an industry in which new capital can be profitably employed. This is not a situation which can be changed by changes in the Administration at Washington. It is a tangible, not a psychological, barrier to new investment and to the consequent further expansion of our industrial plant. The capitalist would welcome a Republican administration, but he would not think of it in terms of his being able to make new investments as much as in terms of his being more certain of a substantial return on the investment he has already made.

It is true that the advent of a Republican administration would result in a tremendous outburst of prosperity propaganda. The band would play and the boys would shout and the editors would nine-tenths of them turn out. Even the Wall Streeter would exert himself to put on a Bull Market, confident in his ability to be the first one out from under in the event of a subsequent crash. A good many small and medium sized business men might be sufficiently moved by the restoration of Republicanism to start new or to expand old enterprises and some measure of reemployment would undoubtedly take place. Meanwhile, every man who went back to work would get a headline whereas the men dropped from relief roles would not get even an obituary.

But whatever immediate "prosperity" might be whipped up to adorn the inaugural of a Republican president would necessarily be a prosperity of a superficial and temporary kind. We have seen that the large corporations can achieve a large measure of new production with a small measure of new employment. A rapid expansion of output (which would be accompanied by a rapid rise in prices) would result only in a repetition of the 1936 recovery and the 1937 slump. The corporations do not need to increase their payrolls in proportion to their increase in production, and they are certainly not going to hire more men without producing more goods. Soon the underlying discrepancy between the ability of the producer to produce and the ability of the consumer to pay for the product would again assert itself. Soon there would be another "recession," but this time it would be blamed not on high taxes but on high wages; not on Roosevelt but on the "Reds," not on the rich man but on the poor.

And if, by some miracle that will never take place, the industrialist should nurse along his recovery so carefully that it might take an apparently permanent root, another boom could only result in another crash and a recurrence of depression and of panic might lead to something more than merely an economic crisis. The industrialist would be indeed desperate if he were again discredited. It might be more difficult to elect a third Roosevelt than it was to elect a second.

In the absence of either a boom or a panic, the trend (under conservative auspices) would be toward a long, slow process of gradual decline. With reduced relief-payments and fewer persons on relief roles, the unemployed would be turned into a tremendous reservoir of cheap man power. Labor leaders would find it constantly more difficult to maintain union wages, or even to preserve the unions themselves as bargaining instruments of any real utility. Every method of influencing public opinion would be applied to spread the conviction that a man should be happy to accept any job, no matter what the pay or what the hours. As wages declined, so also would the prices the farmer received for his crops. In the cities and on the farm the standard of living would be steadily lowered. But, for the time being, the corporations would save more on wages than they would lose on sales and dividends would continue to be paid.

This is a young country, from an economic standpoint. At the time of the Industrial Revolution, it was hardly more than a strip of towns along the seacoast. Its large-scale industry dates only from the close of the Civil War. When we were founding our steel industry, Indians were still on the warpath. Not more than fifty years ago our natural resources were still largely undeveloped, great areas of our country were still largely unsettled. To our grandfathers and to our fathers it must have seemed that our opportunities for expansion were endless, that only a geographical frontier could ever be reached.

Now it is in our relatively new cities, such as Cleveland and Detroit, that depression has struck hardest and unemployment has been most intense. And in the far west, the last part of the continent to be settled, the final reaches of our promised land, state borders are patrolled to keep out newcomers, strangers are not welcome lest they might add to the economic burden of those already within the gates. It is probable that the system of unrestricted individualism through which we developed our industrial civilization was the system best fitted to the time. But it should be evident that conditions have changed, reluctant as we may be to change with them.

From an economic standpoint, we have lost the equality of opportunity on which any philosophy of individualism must necessarily be based. If Mr. Ford were young again, I do not quite see what he could do with himself except get a job in an automobile factory. If Mr. Carnegie had just arrived from Scotland, he would need to have brought a few hundred million dollars with him had he come with any thought of impressing himself upon the steel industry. Our most recent mass-production industry (the radio) was largely developed under the auspices of General Electric and Westinghouse Electric & Manufacturing, the two corporations which controlled most of the basic patents in the field. Mr. David Sarnoff, who in an earlier period might have been the entrepreneur of the wireless, is instead an extremely high-class hired man. The most conspicuous individualism shown in the radio industry was the individualism of various manufacturers who cheerfully manufactured radio parts and sets without paying the slightest attention to the patent law.

As for the small company, its chances of becoming a big company were never less bright. The "little fellow," squeezed between the high prices charged by his suppliers and the low incomes earned by his customers, disappears annually in large numbers and the wonder is that there always seems to be some other optimist to take his place. Even at its best period, our system shone most brightly only when it was judged by its exceptions; there were only a few lucky numbers although they gave the lottery a good name. But now we have even fewer winners and the losers are very much worse off.

In the past, the man of average education, average ability and average character had an excellent chance of finding himself some niche and continuing to occupy it. He never got rich. He was never free from financial worries. He was not what would be considered a success. But neither was he a failure. His job was reasonably secure. As he grew older in it he made a little more money. Eventually he might be awarded a gold watch or a key to the executive's washroom. When he died he was decently buried and his family carried decently on.

Now this man has lost, in a large measure, whatever degree of security he once possessed. He is liable to discharge without warning, through circumstances entirely beyond his control. Many jobs become more precarious the longer they are held, for industrial senility arrives at a constantly lower age. It is no wonder that this man is turning to the Townsend Plan, to Thirty Dollars Every Thursday, or that the demagogue and the medicine man so easily find his attentive ear.

And as for this man's children, they are hardly in a position to repeat even his modest career. Employers do not need to hire beginners nowadays. There are too many experienced men and women out of work.

It is for these reasons that appeals to the American tradition, the American system, the American way have so little meaning today and will have even less tomorrow. It is unfortunate that most of our positions of power and influence are occupied by relatively old men who do not realize that the country in which they are living is not the same as the country in which they were young. It is also unfortunate — although very natural — that the minority who have reached (or inherited) some measure of security and position and wealth have so strong an interest in maintaining the status quo. There is something the matter with individualism when so many individuals find it so difficult to get enough to eat.

Meanwhile our industrial machine staggers onward, with none of the bumps and few of the ditches missed. A good many millions of persons are working, although a good many other millions would like their jobs. Tremendous amounts of energy are still being expended; the earth gives up its coal (to a receiver) and the railroads (with the assistance of the Reconstruction Finance Corporation) continue to run. We live, breathe and have our being, although over all hangs an atmosphere of terror — fear of the job, fear of a war, fear of the future and what the future may bring. It is remarkable how few companies and how few individuals are the beneficiaries of all this. A handful of large corporations — a handful of their large stockholders — for them the seed is planted and the harvest reaped. It does not matter how little the little man prospers. It does not matter how many farmers lose their farms. It does not matter how many people are jobless or how little those who have a job may make. These companies are in no position in our present social economy to deal with such matters — or, indeed, under any obligation to care about them — in a statesmanlike way. They have their profits to look after. They have their dividends to pay.

APPENDIX A

	Corporations Reporting Net Income		Corporations Reporting Defects	
	Number	*Amount*	*Number*	*Amount*
1925	252,300	$9,583,000,000	132,700*	$1,962,000,000
1926	258,100	9,673,000,000	149,400*	2,168,000,000
1927	259,800	9,220,000,000	166,800	2,380,000,000
1928	268,800	10,950,000,000	174,800	2,280,000,000
1929	269,400	11,930,000,000	186,600	2,800,000,000

* Estimated. Government figures include inactive corporations, which have been excluded from following years' figures.

APPENDIX B

	Corporations Reporting Net Income		Corporations Reporting *No* Net Income	
	Number	*Amount*	*Number*	*Amount*
1930	221,400	$6,429,000,000	241,600	$4,877,000,000
1931	175,900	3,683,000,000	283,800	6,971,000,000
1932	82,600	2,153,000,000	369,200	7,796,000,000
1933	109,800	2,986,000,000	337,000	5,533,000,000
1934	145,100	4,275,000,000	324,700	4,181,000,000
1935	164,100	5,149,000,000	312,800	3,451,000,000

APPENDIX C

All Corporations

Year	Number	Net Income
1930	463,000	$1,550,000,000
1931	459,700	def. 3,290,000,000
1932	451,800	def. 5,640,000,000
1933	446,800	def. 2,500,000,000
1934	469,800	94,000,000

Corporations with $1,000,000-&-over Net Income

Year	Number	Net Income
1930	736	$3,700,000,000
1931	409	2,100,000,000
1932	284	1,125,000,000
1933	387	1,540,000,000
1934	580	2,080,000,000

Corporations Except Those with $1,000,000-&-over Net Income

Year	Number	Net Income
1930	462,300	def. $2,150,000,000
1931	459,300	def. 5,390,000,000
1932	451,500	def. 6,765,000,000
1933	446,400	def. 4,090,000,000
1934	469,200	def. 1,986,000,000

APPENDIX D

46 More Companies with 1929 Profit of over $20,000,000 to $40,000,000

(Net Income in Millions)

Cities Service	$39.3	North American Co	28.8
Socony	38.8	Baltimore & Ohio	28.7
International Harvester	36.8	Westinghouse Electric	27.0
Vacuum Oil	36.8	A & P	26.2
Chesapeake & Ohio	36.5	Great Northern	25.6
Union Carbide	36.0	Aluminum Co	25.3
Woolworth	35.6	American & Foreign Power	24.7
Utah Copper	33.6	Prairie Pipe Line	22.8
Philadelphia Co	32.7	American Can	22.7
Electric Bond & Share	32.5	N. Y., New Haven	22.3
Humble Oil	32.5	International Nickel	22.2
United Gas Improvement	32.5	Eastman Kodak	22.0
Reynolds Tobacco	32.2	Liggett & Myers	22.0
Columbia Gas	32.1	Chrysler	21.9
Commonwealth & Southern	30.4	Northern Pacific	21.8
Allied Chemical	30.2	Chile Copper	21.8
American Tobacco	30.2	American Smelting	21.8
Sears, Roebuck	30.0	Curtis Publishing	21.5
Chicago, Burlington & Quincy	29.6	Youngstown Steel	21.5
Public Service of N. J.	29.5	National Biscuit	21.4
Kreuger & Toll	29.1	American Gas	21.2
		Jones & Laughlin	20.8
		International March	20.6
		Borden	20.4
		American Radiator	20.0

APPENDIX E

18 More Companies with 1937 Profit of Over $20,000,000
(Net Income in Millions)

United Gas Improvement............	$29.1	Public Service of N. J.	24.5
Aluminum Co.........	27.8	Phillips Petroleum....	24.1
Reynolds Tobacco....	27.6	Shell Union..........	22.5
Pennsylvania R. R....	27.3	Eastman Kodak......	22.3
Procter & Gamble...	26.8	Chile Copper.........	22.3
American Tobacco....	26.2	Philadelphia Electric..	21.7
Coca-Cola...........	24.7	Liggett & Myers.....	21.4
Allied Chemical......	24.7	Consolidated Oil......	20.8
Pacific Gas..........	24.6	Westinghouse Electric	20.1

INDEX